MW00533414

THE
THOUGHT
OF
CREATION

Kabbalah Publishing is a registered DBA of
The Kabbalah Centre International, Inc.

For further information:

The Kabbalah Centre
155 E. 48th St., New York, NY 10017
1062 S. Robertson Blvd., Los Angeles, CA 90035

1.800.Kabbalah www.kabbalah.com

First Edition, July 2013

Printed in USA

ISBN: 978-1-57189-896-8

Design: HL Design (Hyun Min Lee) www.hldesignco.com

KABBALAH
PUBLISHING

THE
THOUGHT
OF
CREATION

*On the Individual, Humanity, and
Their Ultimate Perfection*

Rav Yehuda Ashlag

EDITED BY MICHAEL BERG

Table of Contents

חלק ראשון: להסתכל במראה

PART THREE: QUANTUM METAPHYSICS

Foreword

I feel extremely privileged and excited to share with you this book from the writings of the greatest kabbalist of our time, Rav Yehuda Ashlag. An important kabbalistic teaching is that we can only receive from a teacher or teaching to the degree that we have appreciation for that teacher or teaching. I hope in this short introduction to awaken within you a true, if only slight, appreciation for this book.

Rav Ashlag would often write an introduction to each of his great works of Kabbalah. This work you are now reading was originally written as an introduction to his complete translation and commentary to the *Zohar*, which he called *HaSulam* (*The Ladder*). Most introductions serve as a short gateway to a book, but Rav Ashlag's introduction takes on a different and much more significant role.

I have had the ultimate blessing to have studied with my father Kabbalist Rav Berg, who received his wisdom from his teacher, Rav Yehuda Brandwein, who was the closest and most devoted student to Rav Ashlag. In a beautiful explanation of their bond, Rav Brandwein writes:

> "All of my teachings are only what I received from my holy teacher, Rav Ashlag, and nothing of my own. I had the merit to serve him for more than thirty two years, and my hand did not leave his hand for all of those years."

Having learned from my father, I believe I have the merit to consider myself, in a small measure, a student of Rav Ashlag and Rav Brandwein.

In one of his letters to my father, Rav Brandwein reveals an important secret concerning Rav Ashlag's introductions. Speaking of Rav Ashlag's introduction to his seminal work, *The Study of the Ten Emanations*, Rav Brandwein writes to my father and teacher Rav Berg:

> "The introduction is deeper then all depths, and you can only truly understand it after you have read and understood all of the sixteen books of *The Study of the Ten Emanations*.

This means that Rav Ashlag infused his introduction to *The Study of the Ten Emanations* with the entirety of the wisdom and Light of the entire work. Therefore, one can comprehend the introduction only after having studied and understood the entire work (which takes years and years of study).

This revelation can begin to open our understanding to the significance of this book you now hold in your hand. In it, Rav Ashlag revealed and infused all of the Light of the entire *Zohar*. We know that the *Zohar* contains the Light that is called the Tree of Life—the Light that has the power to bring an end to all pain, suffering, and death. Therefore, this means that all of that Light is held and concealed within this introduction. This also means that one can understand the great secrets in this book only after one has mastered the entirety of the *Zohar*.

Knowing this, however, should not stop us from reading this book now. Rather, it should grow our appreciation for the great secrets revealed herein. For even though we may know that we are understanding only a fraction of what has been written and revealed, we should also know that this small spark lights brighter much more than we can imagine.

I have been studying this work of Rav Ashlag my entire life, and every time I read it, I discover new secrets. I am sure that as you invest the effort necessary for understanding these elevated words, you will begin to taste and see this book's great Light. One thing I can promise is that, as has been my own experience, once you begin to taste of these secrets, they will change your life forever.

May we all have the merit to taste more and more from the sweetness, beauty, and depth of these teachings and secrets. Most importantly, may we have the merit to see how these elevated words and teachings of the great Kabbalist Rav Ashlag can shape us and our lives.

Blessings,

Michael Berg

Part One:

Looking in the Mirror

חלק ראשון:

להסתכל במראה

Chapter One: Do Not Be Afraid to Ask Difficult Questions

Why should we ask difficult questions?

1. In this introduction, I would like to clarify some seemingly simple matters, that is to say, matters with which everyone occupies themselves, and for the clarification of which much ink has already been used. Nevertheless, [with all these clarifications] we have not yet reached a clear and satisfying understanding of them. Question 1: What is our essence? Question 2: What is our role in the long chain of reality of which we are but small links? Question 3: When we look at ourselves, we feel ourselves to be extremely faulty and low, worthy of nothing but disgrace. Yet when we look upon the Maker Who has formed us, then surely we should be at the peak of virtues, worthy of nothing but praise, because it is certainly expected that from a perfect Architect, only perfect actions can emerge. Question 4: According to reasoning, since He is good and the Provider of goodness Who has no one above Him, how is it that to start with He created so many beings who will experience suffering and agony throughout their lives? After all, the nature of the Good is to bestow goodness and in any case, not to cause so much bad. Question 5: How is it possible that He Who is Eternal, Who has no beginning and no end, would give rise to created beings that live, die, and decay?

2. In order to fully understand all these questions completely, we have to first start with some inquiries, but we should not, Heaven forbid, inquire into those forbidden areas, namely into the Essence of the Creator, which no thought can conceive of at all and of Whom, therefore, we don't have any thought of or word for at all. Rather, we will inquire in those areas where it is a Precept; that is, an inquiry about His actions, as we are required to do according to the Torah: "Know the Creator of your father and serve Him." (1 Chronicles 28:9) And this is also said in *Shir HaYichud* (the Song of Unification): "We have come to know You [the Creator] from Your actions."

פֶּרֶק רִאשׁוֹן: לֹא לְפַחֵד מִשְּׁאֵלוֹת קָשׁוֹת

למה לשאול שאלות קשות?

א) רצוני בהקדמה זו, לברר איזה דברים פשוטים לכאורה, כלומר, אשר ידי הכל ממשמשות בהם, והרבה דיו נשפכה בכדי לבררם. ובכל זאת, עדיין לא הגענו בהם לידי ידיעה ברורה ומספקת. שאלה א) מה מהותנו. שאלה ב) מה תפקידנו בשלשלת המציאות הארוכה, שאנו טבעות קטנות קטנות הימנה. שאלה ג) הנה כשאנו מסתכלים על עצמנו אנו מרגישים את עצמנו, מקולקלים ושפלים עד שאין כמונו לגנות. וכשאנו מסתכלים על הפועל שעשה אותנו, הרי אנו מחויבים להמצא ברום המעלות שאין כמוהו לשבח, כי הכרח הוא, שמפועל השלם תצאנה פעולות שלמות. ד) לפי שהשכל מחייב, הלא הוא ית׳ הטוב ומטיב שאין למעלה הימנו ית׳ *יתברך* ואיך ברא מלכתחילה כל כך הרבה בריות שתתענינה ותתיסרנה בכל ימי היותן, והלא מדרך הטוב להטיב, ועכ״פ *ועל כל פנים* לא להרע כל כך. ה) איך אפשר שמהנצחי שאין לו ראשית ואין לו תכלית, תמשכנה בריות הוות וכלות ונפסדות.

ב) ובכדי לברר כל זה בשלמות. צריכים אנו להקדים איזו חקירות, ולא ח״ו *חס ושלום* במקום האסור, דהיינו בעצמותו של הבורא ית׳ *יתברך*, אשר לית מחשבה תפיסא בו כלל וכלל, ואין לנו משום זה שום מחשבה והגה בו ית׳. אלא במקום שהחקירה היא מצוה, דהיינו החקירה במעשיו ית׳, כמצוה לנו בתורה, דע את אלקי אביך ועבדהו (דברי הימים א, כח׳, ט׳), וכן אומר בשיר היחוד ממעשיך הכרנוך.

The first inquiry is: How can we imagine that creation could be like new, which means something new that was not included within Him (the Creator) before He created it, when it is clear to any person with a clear mind that there is nothing that is not included in Him? This is something that common sense, too, compels us to conclude, for is there anyone who can give you something that he does not have within himself? The second inquiry [asks]: If you want to say that as far as His omnipotence is concerned, it is certain that He can create something out of nothing, that is, a new thing that has no existence in Him, then the question arises, what sort of reality is it, that can be decided upon, that did not exist [lit. had no place] within Him but rather is new?

The third inquiry: concerns the saying of the kabbalists that the soul of [every] human being is a part of the Creator from Above (Job, 31:2), in such a way that there is no difference between Him and the soul, only that He is the "whole" and the soul is a "part." [The kabbalists] compared this to a stone that is quarried from a mountain, where there is no difference between the stone and the mountain except for the fact that one is the "whole" and the other is a "part." Therefore we need to investigate further: In the case of a stone that is separated from the mountain, it is indeed separated from the mountain using an ax prepared for this purpose, which separates the "part" from the "whole," but how can one imagine this with regard to Him [the Creator], that He would separate a part of His Essence to the point that it would be outside of His Essence and would become a "part" separate from Him, meaning a soul, so that it can be perceived only as a part of His Essence.

3. The fourth inquiry: Since the chariot of the *Sitra Achra* (Other Side or Impurity) and of the *klipot* (shells) is as distant from the Creator's Holiness as can possibly be, to the point that such distance is altogether beyond our ability to imagine, how is it possible for it [the *Sitra Achra*] to be formed and to extend from the Holiness [of the Creator]? Furthermore, that His Holiness sustains it.

והנה חקירה הא' היא, איך יצויר לנו שהבריאה תהיה מחודשת, שפירושו דבר חדש שלא יהיה כלול בו ית' מטרם שבראו, בו בעת שברור לכל בעל עיון, שאין לך דבר שלא יהיה כלול בו ית', וכן השכל הפשוט מחייב. כי כלום יש לך נותן מה שאין בו. חקירה הב', אם תמצא לומר שמבחינת כל יכלתו, ודאי הוא, שיכול לברוא יש מאין, דהיינו דבר חדש שאין לו שום מציאות בו ית'. נשאלת השאלה, מה היא מציאות הזו, שיתכן להחליט עליה, שאין לה שום מקום בו ית', אלא היא מחודשת.

חקירה הג', במה שאמרו המקובלים, שנשמתו של אדם היא חלק אלוה ממעל (איוב, לא, ב'), באופן שאין הפרש בינו ית' יתברך לבין הנשמה, אלא שהוא ית' "כל", והנשמה "חלק". והמשילו זה לאבן הנחצבת מהר, שאין הפרש בין האבן לבין ההר אלא שזה "כל" וזו "חלק". ולפי"ז ולפי זה יש לחקור, הא תינח, אבן הנחלקת מהר שהיא נפרדת מההר על ידי גרזן המוכן לכך, ונפרד על ידו ה"חלק" מה"כל". אבל איך יצויר זה בו ית' וית', שיפריד חלק מן עצמותו ית', עד שיצא מעצמותו ית' ויהיה "חלק" נבדל הימנו, דהיינו לנשמה, עד שיתכן להבינה רק כחלק מעצמותו ית'.

ג) חקירה הד', כיון שמרכבת הס"א הסטרא אחרא, הצד האחר והקליפות רחוקה מקדושתו ית' יתברך מהקצה אל הקצה, עד שלא תצויר הרחקה כזאת, איך אפשר שתתמשך ותתהוה מהקדושה ית'. ולא עוד אלא שקדושתו ית' תקיים אותה.

The fifth inquiry: concerns the subject of the Resurrection of the Dead. The body is such a despicable thing that it is destined for death and for burial from the moment of its birth. Moreover, the *Zohar* says that before the body is fully decomposed—as long as there is the slightest remnant of it—the soul cannot ascend to its place in paradise. If this is so, why is it necessary for the body to be revived for the Resurrection of the Dead? Can the Creator not fulfill the souls without it [the body]? And even more puzzling is the statement by the sages that the dead will be resurrected with all their bodily flaws so that no one will be able to say it is someone else, and after that, He will cure their blemishes (*Kohelet Raba* 1:4). We must understand why the Creator should be concerned so much that they will say [about] that [person] that he is someone else, to the point where He would recreate their blemishes and would then be required to cure them.

The sixth inquiry: concerns what [the sages] said that the human being is the center of the entire reality and that all the Supernal Worlds as well as this physical world, including everything that is in them, were fundamentally created only for him (*Zohar, Tazria* 48). "And they obliged [every] person to believe that the world was created for him." (*Sanhedrin* 37) This is seemingly difficult to comprehend: That the Creator bothered to create all of this for him—for this puny human who is not worth the value of even a single hair when compared to the value of the existence of this world, and how much less so when compared to the Supernal Worlds, which are infinite in scope and exaltedness. And furthermore, what does one need all of this for?

Who acts without a purpose?

4. In order to understand all these questions and inquiries, the one solution [lit. scheme] is to look at the outcome of the action, that is, at the purpose of Creation because it is not possible to understand a thing while it is in the middle of its making but only from its conclusion. And it is clear that no one acts without a purpose because only someone who is out of his mind would act

חקירה הה', ענין תחית המתים. כיון שהגוף הוא דבר בזוי כל כך, עד שתכף מעת לידתו נידון למיתה וקבורה. ולא עוד, אלא שאמרו בזהר, שמטרם שהגוף נרקב כולו, לא תוכל הנשמה לעלות למקומה לגן עדן, כל עוד שיש איזה שיור הימנו. וא"כ ואם כן מהו החיוב, שיחזור ויקום לתחית המתים, וכי לא יוכל הקב"ה הקדוש ברוך הוא לענג את הנשמות בלעדו. ויותר תמוה מ"ש מה שאמרו חז"ל, שעתידים המתים לקום לתחיה במומם, כדי שלא יאמרו אחר הוא (מדרש קוהלת רבה, א', ד'), ואח"ז ואחרי זה ירפא את המומים שלהם. ויש להבין, מה איכפת לו להקב"ה שיאמרו אחר הוא. עד שבשביל זה הוא יחזור ויברא את המום שבהם, ויוצרך לרפואתם.

חקירה הו', במה שאמרו [חכמינו] ז"ל, אשר האדם הוא מרכז כל המציאות, שכל העולמות העליונים ועוה"ז העולם הזה הגשמי וכל מלואם, לא נבראו אלא בשבילו (זהר תזריע מ"ח) וחייבו את האדם להאמין שבשבילו נברא העולם (סנהדרין לז). שלכאורה קשה להבין, שבשביל האדם הקטן הזה, שאינו תופס ערך של שערה בערך מציאות העוה"ז העולם הזה, ומכ"ש ומכל שכן בערך כל העולמות העליונים שאין קץ להם ולרוממותם, טרח הקב"ה לברוא כל אלו בשבילו. וכן, למה לו לאדם כל זה.

האם מישהו פועל ללא מטרה וללא תכלית?

ד) ובכדי להבין כל אלו השאלות והחקירות, תחבולה האחת היא להסתכל בסוף המעשה, כלומר בתכלית הבריאה. כי אי אפשר להבין שום דבר באמצע מלאכתו, אלא מסופו. וזה ברור הוא, שאין לך פועל בלי תכלית, כי רק מי שאינו שפוי בדעתו, תמצאהו פועל

without a purpose. I know that there are those who pretend to be wise, who have rebelled against the Torah and the Precepts, who say that the Creator created the entire reality and then left it to itself. [They even say that] it is because of the insignificance of His created beings that it does not behoove the Creator, Who is so high and exalted, to look over their petty and disgraceful ways.

Indeed, they do not speak out of wisdom because it is not possible to decide about our inferiority and unworthiness before we conclude that we formed ourselves, and that we created all the spoiled and despicable nature of ours. However, at the same time, if we conclude that the Creator Himself, Who is perfect in all possible perfection, is the Artisan Who has created and engineered our bodies, with all their good as well as despicable inclinations, [we should know] that a Perfect Maker would never create a contemptible and faulty product. And any action is a testimony to the quality of its maker, so what blame should be assigned to a faulty garment if a bad tailor made it?

In a similar vein of study (in Tractate *Ta'anit* 20) a story is told about Rav Elazar, son of Rav Shimon bar Yochai, etc., who came across a person who was exceedingly ugly, etc. [Rav Elazar] said to him, "How ugly you are, etc." And [the ugly] man answered him, "Go and tell the Artisan who made me: How ugly is the vessel that You have created, etc." Study that well. Those who are wise in their own eyes and say: "Because of our lowliness and insignificance, it does not behoove the Creator to supervise over us and that He has left us"—thereby only declare their own foolishness.

Just imagine... Suppose you met someone who has found a way to create living beings with a predetermined *kavanah* (meditation) for them to suffer and experience agony throughout their lives, just as we do. And furthermore, once he created them, he would carelessly abandon them without even wanting to supervise over them in order to give them a little help. How greatly would you denounce and disregard this person? Is it possible to imagine such a thing about the Source of Existence—the Creator Himself?

בלי תכלית. ויודע אני שיש מתחכמים פורקי עול תורה ומצות, שאומרים, שהבורא ית' יתברך ברא את כל המציאות ועזב אותה לנפשה, כי מחמת האפסיות שבאלו הבריות, אינו מתאים לבורא ית' לרוב רוממותו, להשגיח על דרכיהן הפעוטות והמגונות.

אכן לא מדעת דברו זאת, כי לא יתכן להחליט על שפלותנו ואפסותנו, מטרם שנחליט, שאנחנו עשינו את עצמנו ואת כל אלו הטבעים המקולקלים והמגונים שבנו. אבל בה בעת שאנו מחליטים, אשר הבורא ית' השלם בכל השלמות, הוא בעל המלאכה שברא ותיכן את גופותנו, על כל נטיות הטובות והמגונות שבהם, הרי מתחת יד הפועל השלם לא תצא לעולם פעולה בזויה ומקולקלת, וכל פעולה מעידה על טיב פועלה, ומה אשמתו של בגד מקולקל, אם איזה חייט לא יוצלח תפר אותו?

ועי' כגון זה (במס' תענית כ') מעשה שבא ר"א רבי אלעזר בר"ש בן רבי שמעון וכו' נזדמן לו אדם אחד, שהיה מכוער ביותר וכו', אמר לו כמה מכוער אותו האיש וכו', אמר לו לך ואמור לאומן שעשאני: כמה מכוער כלי זה שעשית וכו' עש"ה עיין שם היטב. הרי שמתחכמים אלו לומר, שמסבת שפלותנו ואפסותנו אין מתאים לו ית' להשגיח עלינו, ועזב אותנו, הם אינם אלא מכריזים על חוסר דעתם בלבד.

ודמה לך. אם היית פוגש איזה אדם, שימציא לו לברא בריות מלכתחילה, בכדי שתתענינה ותתיסרנה בכל ימי חייהם כמונו, ולא עוד אלא להשליך אותן אחר גיוו מבלי שירצה אפילו להשגיח בהן, כדי לעזרן מעט, כמה היית מגנה ומזלזל בו. והיתכן להעלות על הדעת כזה על מחויב המציאות ית' וית'.

5. And therefore, common sense obligates us to understand that the [truth] is the opposite of what is superficially apparent. And we should establish that we are, in fact, very good and highly evolved beings to the point where there is no end to our importance—exactly as befits the Craftsman Who made us. Because any flaw or fault that you would like to attribute to our bodies, no matter what reasons and excuses you might find, ends up being attributed to the Creator Who created us and our entire nature.

It is evident that He made us rather than we made ourselves. And He also knew all the consequences that could extend and emerge from all those natural and evil inclinations that He put in us. But this is why we said that we need to look at the final outcome of the action because then we can understand everything. And it is a common saying known all over: Do not show a fool something in the middle of its creation.

What does the Creator want from us?

6. And our sages have already instructed us (see [in the book] *Tree of Life, Gate of Vessels*, at the beginning of Chapter 1) that the Creator created the world solely to bestow pleasure upon His created beings. And it is here where we need to cast our eyes and all of our thoughts because this was the ultimate *kavanah* (meditation) and action of creating the world. And we have to look into it: Since the Thought of Creation was to bestow pleasure upon His created beings, it necessarily follows that He would have created a great deal of desire in their souls to receive that which He thought to bestow upon them.

After all, the amount of every delight and pleasure is measured by the degree of the Desire to Receive it [the pleasure]. So as much as the Desire to Receive is greater, then to that extent is the degree of the pleasure much greater, and as much as the Desire to Receive it [the pleasure] is smaller, then to that same degree the amount of pleasure from receiving is reduced.

ה) ולפיכך השכל הבריא מחייב אותנו להבין, את ההיפך מהנראה בשטחיות, ולהחליט שאנו באמת בריות טובות ונעלות ביותר, עד שאין קץ לחשיבותנו, דהיינו ממש באופן הראוי והמתאים לבעל מלאכה שעשה אותנו. כי כל משהו חסרון שתרצה להרהר על גופותנו, הנה אחר כל מיני תירוצים שאתה מתרץ לך, הוא נופל רק על הבורא ית', שברא אותנו ואת כל הטבעים שבנו.

שהרי ברור, שהוא עשנו ולא אנחנו, גם ידע כל אלו התהלוכות, אשר תמשכנה לצאת מכל אלו הטבעיות והנטיות הרעות שנטע בנו. אלא הוא הדבר אשר אמרנו, שצריכים אנו להסתכל על סוף המעשה. ואז נוכל להבין הכל. ומשל בפי העולם, אל תראה דבר לשוטה באמצע מלאכתו.

מה הבורא רוצה מאתנו?

ו) וכבר הורונו חז"ל (עי' ע"ח עיין [בספר] עץ חיים שער הכלים פ"א פרק א' בתחילתו), שלא ברא הקב"ה את העולם אלא בכדי להנות לנבראיו. וכאן אנו צריכים להשים את עינינו וכל מחשבותינו, כי הוא סוף הכונה והמעשה של בריאת העולם. ויש להתבונן, כיון שמחשבת הבריאה היתה בכדי להנות לנבראיו, הרי הכרח הוא, שברא בנשמות מדת רצון גדולה עד מאד, לקבל את אשר חשב ליתן להן.

שהרי מדת גדלו של כל תענוג וכל הנאה, מדודה במדת גדלו של הרצון לקבל אותו, עד שכל שהרצון לקבל גדול יותר, הנה בשיעור הזה מדת התענוג גדולה ביותר, וכל שהרצון לקבלו פחות יותר, הרי באותה המדה נפחת שעור התענוג מהקבלה.

It follows that the very Thought of Creation would require creating in the souls an extremely exaggerated Desire to Receive that would be equivalent to the degree of the great pleasure with which the Almighty had thought to delight the souls. This is because the great pleasure and the great Desire to Receive go hand in hand.

7) After learning all this, we have come to fully understand the second inquiry, so that it is absolutely resolved. We have inquired to know what reality is there, that can be clearly decided upon as not existing and not included within His Essence, so much so that it can be referred to as a new Creation—Something from Nothing. And now that we have come to clearly know that the Thought of Creation was to give pleasure to His created beings, He of necessity had created a degree of Desire in order to receive from Him all this pleasure and goodness that He had planned for them. And this Desire to Receive was surely not present in His Essence before the souls were created, for whom could He have received from? Thus, it follows that He created something new, [something] that was not in His Essence.

Moreover, it is understood that according to the Thought of Creation, it was unnecessary to create anything other than this Desire to Receive because this new Creation was already sufficient for fulfilling the entire Thought of Creation, [fulfillment] which He thought to give us pleasure with. But the entire fulfillment included in the Thought of Creation—that is to say, all the pleasures that He had planned for us—extend directly from His Essence, and He has no need to create them anew, as they are already extending [from His essence], as Something out of Something, towards the great Desire to Receive that exists in the souls. And, with this, it has been made absolutely clear to us that the entire substance of this Creation anew, from beginning to end, is simply this Desire to Receive.

הרי שמחשבת הבריאה בעצמה, מחייבת בהכרח לברוא בנשמות רצון לקבל בשיעור מופרז ביותר, המתאים למדת התענוג הגדול, שכל יכלתו חשב לענג את הנשמות. כי התענוג הגדול והרצון לקבל הגדול עולים בקנה אחד.

ז) ואחר שידענו זה, כבר הגענו להבין חקירה הב' עד סופה בבירור מוחלט. כי חקרנו לדעת מה היא המציאות שאפשר להחליט עליה בבירור, שאינה מצויה ואינה נכללת בעצמותו ית' עד שנאמר שהיא בריאה מחודשת יש מאין. ועתה שידענו בבירור, שמחשבת הבריאה, שהיא בכדי להנות לנבראיו, בראה בהכרח מדת רצון, לקבל ממנו ית' את כל הנועם והטוב הזה שחשב בעדם, הנה הרצון לקבל הזה, ודאי שלא היה כלול בעצמותו ית' מטרם שבראו בנשמות, כי ממי יקבל? הרי שברא דבר מחודש, שאינו בו ית'.

ויחד עם זה, מובן על פי מחשבת הבריאה, שלא היה צריך כלל לברוא משהו יותר מהרצון לקבל הזה, שהרי בריאה מחודשת הזו כבר מספקת לו ית' למלאות כל מחשבת הבריאה שחשב עלינו להנות אותנו. אבל כל המלוי שבמחשבת הבריאה, דהיינו כל מיני הטבות שחשב בעדנו, כבר הן נמשכות בהמשכה ישרה מעצמותו ית' ואין לו ענין לברוא אותן מחדש, בעת שכבר הן נמשכות יש מיש אל הרצון לקבל הגדול שבנשמות. והנה נתברר לנו בהחלט שכל החומר כולו מתחילתו עד סופו, שבבריאה המחודשת, הוא רק "הרצון לקבל".

What is the source of negativity in this world?

8. And this brings us to the understanding of the idea that the kabbalists had in mind, [the one] which we raised in the third inquiry. Since we were wondering about them, how is it possible to say about the souls that they are part of the Divine Above—like being compared to a stone quarried from a mountain—where there is no difference between them except that one of them is a "part" and the other is the "whole"?

We wondered: it is understandable that the stone was severed from the mountain through the use of an ax that was especially made for this purpose. But when we talk about His Essence, how is it possible to say such a thing and what tool is there [that can] separate the souls from the Creator's Essence so that they cease being the Creator and become created beings? From what has been explained, it has become very clear that just as the ax cuts through a material object and divides it into two, so also Difference of Form separates within the spiritual realm and divides it into two.

For example, when two people love each other, you would say that they cleave to each other as one body. And on the other hand, when they hate each other, you would say that they are as far from each other as East is from West. This is not a matter of proximity or distance. Rather, the meaning refers to Similarity of Form: When they are similar in form to each other—one loves all that his friend loves and hates all that his friend hates, and so on—they are considered as loving each other and cleaving to each other.

But if there is any Difference of Form between them, that is, that one loves something although his friend hates that thing, and so on, then to the degree that this Difference of Form exists, they hate each other and are distant from each other. And if, for example, they are completely opposite in form [from each other], in which case everything one person loves is found to be hated by his friend and everything that he hates is found to be loved by the other, then they are as far from each other as East is from West—in other words, as from one extreme to the other.

מאין באה השליליות לעולם?

ח) ומכאן באנו גם לסוף דעתם של המקובלים, שהבאנו בחקירה הג'. שתמהנו עליהם, איך אפשר לומר על הנשמות, שהן חלק אלקי ממעל, בהשואה אל האבן שנחצבה מהר, שאין הפרש ביניהן אלא שזה "חלק" וזה "כל".

ותמהנו, תינח האבן שנפרדה מההר, שנעשית חלקו על ידי גרזן מוכן לכך, אבל בעצמותו ית' איך יתכן לומר כזה, ובמה נחלקו הנשמות מעצמותו ית' ויצאו מכלל בורא ית' להיות נבראים. ובהמתבאר מובן הדבר היטב, כי כמו שהגרזן מחתך ומבדיל בדבר גשמי לחלקהו לשנים. כן שינוי הצורה מבדיל ברוחני לחלקהו לשנים.

למשל כשב' אנשים אוהבים זה את זה, תאמר שהם דבקים זה בזה כגוף אחד. ולהיפך כשהם שונאים זה את זה, תאמר שהם רחוקים איש מרעהו כרחוק מזרח ממערב. ואין כאן ענין של קרבת מקום או ריחוק מקום, אלא הכונה היא על השתוות הצורה, שבהיותם שוים בצורתם איש לרעהו, שאוהב כל מה שחברו אוהב ושונא כל מה שחברו שונא וכדומה. נמצאים אוהבים זה את זה ודבוקים זה בזה.

ואם יש ביניהם איזה שינוי צורה . דהיינו שאוהב דבר מה, אע"פ ואף עלפי שחברו שונא הדבר, וכדומה, הרי בשיעור שינוי הצורה הזה, הם שונאים ורחוקים זה מזה. ואם למשל הם בהפכיות הצורה, דהיינו כל מה שזה אוהב נמצא שנוא לחברו, וכל מה שזה שונא נמצא אהוב לחברו, הרי אז רחוקים זה מזה כרחוק מזרח ממערב, דהיינו מקצה אל הקצה.

9. And thus, you find that in the spiritual [world] Difference of Form functions just as an ax is used to separate things in the physical world, and that the degree of distance is equivalent to the degree of the Difference of Form. And, from this, you can learn that once the Desire to Receive His pleasure had been deeply planted in the souls, as was mentioned and proven above, this form [Desire to Receive] did not exist at all in the Creator because, Heaven forbid, from whom could He receive? Hereby, it is this Difference of Form [Desire to Receive] that the souls received, which acted to separate them from His Essence, just as an ax separates the stone from the mountain. This happened in such a way that through this Difference of Form, the souls ceased being a Creator and were separated from Him to become created beings.

Indeed, whatever the souls obtain from the Light of the Creator is an extension—Something out of Something—from His Essence. Therefore, it is found that from the aspect of His Light that is received in the Vessel that is within them, which is the Desire to Receive, there is no difference at all between them and His Essence because they are receiving Something out of Something directly from His Essence; and thus, the entire difference between the souls and His Essence is merely that the souls are a part of His Essence.

This means that the degree of Light they receive into the Vessel, which is the Desire to Receive, is already a distinct part of the Divine because it is contained within the Difference of Form of the Desire to Receive. For it is this Difference of Form that has made [the Vessel] a "part," and through this, it has come out of the aspect of the "whole" and has become a "part." So, there is no difference between them [the Divine and the soul] except that one is the "whole" and the other is a "part," like a mountain and the stone cut from it. Contemplate on this well because one cannot say more on such a Supernal issue.

ט) והנך מוצא, שברוחניות פועל שינוי הצורה כמו גרזן מפריד בין הגשמים, וכן שיעור ההרחקה כפי שיעור הפכיות הצורה. ומכאן תשכיל, כיון שנטבע בנשמות הרצון לקבל הנאתו כנ"ל אשר הוכחנו בעליל, שצורה זו אינה נמצאת כלל בהבורא ית' יתברך, כי ח"ו חס ושלום ממי יקבל, הרי שינוי צורה הזה, שהשיגו הנשמות, פועל להפרידם מעצמותו ית', כדמיון הגרזן החוצב האבן מן ההר. באופן שע"י שינוי הצורה הזה יצאו הנשמות מכלל בורא, ונבדלו הימנו להיות נבראים.

אמנם כל מה שמשיגות הנשמות מאורו ית', הרי הוא נמשך יש מי שמעצמותו ית'. א"כ אם כן נמצא, שמבחינת אורו ית' שמקבלות תוך הכלי שבהן, שהוא הרצון לקבל, אין הפרש כלל ביניהן לעצמותו ית', שהרי מקובל להן יש ישר מעצמותו ית', וכל ההפרש שבין הנשמות לעצמותו ית', אינו יותר, אלא במה שהנשמות הן חלק מעצמותו ית'.

דהיינו ששיעור האור שקבלו תוך הכלי שהוא הרצון לקבל, כבר הוא חלק נבדל מאלקי, בהיותו נשוא תוך שינוי הצורה של הרצון לקבל, ששינוי צורה זה עשה אותה לחלק, שעל ידו יצאו מבחי' "כל" ונעשו לבחינת חלק. הרי שאין ביניהם אלא שזה "כל" וזה חלק, כאבן הנחצבת מהר. והתבונן היטב כי אי אפשר להאריך יותר במקום גבוה כזה.

Why does the Creator allow chaos to exist?

10) And now the gateway has been opened for us to understand the fourth inquiry: How could it be that the Chariot of Impurity and the *klipot* (shells) are formed from His Holiness, since they are far apart from His Holiness, as from one extreme to the other? And how is it possible that He nourishes and sustains them? Here it is necessary first to understand what the essence of the existence of Impurity and the *klipot* (shells) are.

You should know that this great Desire to Receive that we have described—which is the essential being of the souls from the aspect of the very essence of their creation, because they are prepared to receive the entire fulfillment [intended] in the Thought of Creation—does not remain in this same form in the souls. Because had it remained in this form in them, they would have always been forced to be separated from the Creator, since the Difference of Form in them would have separated them from Him. So to repair the problem of this separation, which is placed upon the Vessel of the souls, the Creator created all the Worlds and separated them into two systems, according to the secret meaning of the scriptural passage: "The Creator has made them one in opposition to the other." These are the Four Worlds of Holiness of *Atzilut* (Emanation), *Beriah* (Creation), *Yetzirah* (Formation), and *Asiyah* (Action); and opposed to them are the Four Worlds of *Atzilut*, *Beriah*, *Yetzirah* and *Asiyah* of Impurity.

The Creator stamped the Desire to Share in the system of the Four Worlds of *Atzilut* (Emanation), *Beriah* (Creation), *Yetzirah* (Formation), and *Asiyah* (Action) of Holiness, and removed the Desire to Receive for the Self Alone from them (as was mentioned in the [book]: *Opening to the Wisdom of the Kabbalah*, from verse 14 to verse 19; study this well). And He instilled it [the Desire to Receive for the Self Alone] in the system of the [Four] Worlds of *Atzilut*, *Beriah*, *Yetzirah* and *Asiyah* of Impurity. And because of this, they are separated from the Creator and from all the Worlds of Holiness. For this reason, the *klipot* (shells) are referred to as dead,

למה הבורא מאפשר לכאוס להתקיים?

יוד) ועתה נפתח לנו הפתח להבין החקירה הד'. איך אפשר שיתהוה מקדושתו ית' ענין מרכבת הטומאה והקליפות, אחר שהיא רחוקה מקדושתו ית' מקצה אל הקצה, ואיך יתכן שיפרנס אותה ויקיימה. אכן יש להבין מקודם ענין מציאות מהות הטומאה והקליפות מה היא.

ותדע, שזה הרצון לקבל הגדול, שאמרנו, שהוא עצם מהותן של הנשמות מבחינה עצם בריאתן, כי ע"כ על כן הן מוכנות לקבל כל המלוי שבמחשבת הבריאה, הוא לא נשאר בצורתו זו בנשמות, כי אם היה נשאר בהן, היו מוכרחות להשאר תמיד בפרודא ממנו ית', כי שינוי הצורה שבהן היה מפרידן ממנו ית'. ובכדי לתקן דבר הפירוד הזה, המונח על הכלי של הנשמות, ברא ית' את כל העולמות כולם, והבדילם לב' מערכות, בסו"ה זה לעומת זה עשה אלקים, שהן ד' עולמות אבי"ע אצילות, בריאה, יצירה, עשיה דקדושה, ולעומתם ד' עולמות אבי"ע אצילות, בריאה, יצירה, עשיה דטומאה.

והטביע את הרצון להשפיע במערכת אבי"ע אצילות, בריאה, יצירה, עשיה דקדושה, והסיר מהם את הרצון לקבל לעצמו, (כמ"ש כמו שכתוב להלן בפתיחה לחכמת הקבלה מאות י"ד עד אות י"ט עש"ה עיין שם היטב). ונתן אותו במערכת העולמות אבי"ע אצילות, בריאה, יצירה, עשיה דטומאה, ונמצאו בגללו נפרדים מהבורא ית' ומכל העולמות דקדושה. ומטעם זה מכונות הקליפות בשם מתים כמ"ש כמו שכתוב

as is said in the Scriptures: "sacrifices of the dead" (Psalms 106:28) and the same applies to the wicked who are attracted to them, as our sages have said: "The wicked are called dead, even when they are still alive. (Tractate *Berachot* 15b)"

Since the Desire to Receive that was instilled in them by their Opposite of Form from [the Creator's] Holiness separates them from the Life of the living; and they are far apart from Him, as from one extreme to the other, because He has no aspect of receiving whatsoever, only in bestowing. However, the *klipot* (shells) have no aspect of sharing whatsoever, only in receiving for their own pleasure alone, and there is no greater divergence than this. And you already know that spiritual distance starts with some Difference of Form and ends up with a complete Opposite of Form, which is the ultimate distance, until the last iota.

11) The Worlds have been gradually evolved and unfolded all the way to the reality of this physical world, that is, to a place in which there is an existence for a body and a soul, and also a period of damage and *tikkun* (correction). This is because the body, which is the Desire to Receive for the Self Alone, extends from its root in the Thought of Creation, as mentioned above, and passes through the system of the Worlds of Impurity, as is said in the scriptural passage: "A man is born like a wild ass's colt," (Job 11:12) and he remains enslaved under that system up to the age of 13, and this is [the period that is referred to as] the period of damage.

By engaging with the Precepts [of the Torah] from the age of 13 years onward—engagement for the purpose of giving pleasure to his Maker—the person starts to purify the Desire to Receive for the Self Alone that is ingrained in him, and slowly and gradually transforms it into [the Desire to Receive] for the Sake of Sharing. Through this, he draws the *Nefesh* (Lower Soul) of Holiness from its source in the Thought of Creation; and she [the *Nefesh*] passes through the system of the Worlds of Holiness and is [then] clothed in a body, and this is the period of the *tikkun* (correction).

זבחי מתים (תהילים קו', כח'), וכן הרשעים הנמשכים אחריהם, כמ"ש
כמו שאמרו חז"ל הרשעים בחייהם נקראים מתים (מסכת ברכות, דף טו', ב').

כי הרצון לקבל המוטבע בהם בהפכיות הצורה מקדושתו ית'
מפרידן מחיי החיים, והן רחוקות ממנו ית' מקצה אל הקצה, כי
הוא ית' אין לו שום ענין של קבלה אלא רק להשפיע לבד, והקליפות
אין להן שום ענין של השפעה רק לקבל לעצמן להנאתן בלבד, ואין
הפכיות גדולה מזה. וכבר ידעת, שהמרחק הרוחני מתחיל בשינוי
צורה במשהו ומסתיים בהפכיות הצורה, שהיא סוף המרחק
בדיוטא האחרונה.

יא) ונשתלשלו העולמות עד למציאות עולם הזה הגשמי, דהיינו
למקום שתהיה בו מציאות גוף ונשמה, וכן זמן קלקול ותיקון,
כי הגוף שהוא הרצון לקבל לעצמו, נמשך משורשו שבמחשבת
הבריאה, כנ"ל, ועובר דרך המערכה של העולמות דטומאה, כמ"ש
כמו שכתוב עייר פרא אדם יולד (איוב יא', יב'), ונשאר משועבד תחת
המערכה ההיא עד י"ג שנה, והוא זמן הקלקול.

ועל ידי עסק המצות מי"ג שנים ואילך, שעוסק על מנת להשפיע
נחת רוח ליוצרו, הוא מתחיל לטהר הרצון לקבל לעצמו המוטבע
בו, ומהפכו לאט לאט על מנת להשפיע, שבזה הולך וממשיך נפש
קדושה משורשה במחשבת הבריאה, והיא עוברת דרך המערכה
של העולמות דקדושה והיא מתלבשת בגוף, והוא הזמן של התקון.

And so the person keeps on gaining and attaining stages of holiness from the Thought of Creation in the *Ein Sof* (Endless) until they help him, the person, transform the Desire to Receive for the Self Alone in him, so that it will be completely in the aspect of Receiving for the Sake of Bestowing pleasure to his Maker and not at all for his own benefit. This is how he gains Similarity of Form with his Maker.

Because Receiving for the Sake of Bestowing is considered to be a form of pure Bestowing--(as is mentioned in Tractate *Kidushin*, page 7, about a [spiritually] important person where **she** gives [the ring] and **he** says [the blessing] then this woman is sanctified. [This action is valid] because his receiving that is for the sake of giving pleasure to her who gave [the ring] to him is considered bestowing and complete sharing to her, study that well)--thus gaining complete Cleaving to the Creator because spiritual Cleaving is nothing but Similarity of Form. (As our sages said: How is it possible to cleave to Him? It is only by cleaving to His attributes. Study that Tractate *Shabbat* 133b.) And in this way, a person becomes worthy of receiving all the goodness and the pleasure and the pleasantness in the Thought of Creation.

What was a negative power created for?

12) And hereby the issue of the correction of the Desire to Receive that is ingrained in the souls as part of the Thought of Creation has been thoroughly clarified. The Creator has prepared for them the said two systems [that is, the Worlds of Holiness and the Worlds of Impurity], one in opposition to the other. And through them [these two systems] the souls pass and are divided into two aspects, body and soul, where one [the soul] is clothed with the other. And through the Torah and the Precepts, they [the souls] are found at their conclusion, transforming the Desire to Receive to be like the form of the Desire to Share, and then they can receive all the goodness in the Thought of Creation. At the same time, they merit a strong cleaving to the Creator because through their labor in the Torah and the Precepts, they have merited the Similarity of Form to their Maker, which is considered the End of the *Tikkun* (Correction).

וכן מוסיף והולך לקנות ולהשיג מדרגות דקדושה ממחשבת הבריאה שבא"ס ב"ה שבאין סוף ברוך הוא, עד שהן מסייעות לו להאדם, להפוך את הרצון לקבל לעצמו שבו, שיהיה כולו בבחינת מקבל על מנת להשפיע נחת רוח ליוצרו, ולא כלל לתועלת עצמו, שבזה קונה האדם השואת הצורה ליוצרו.

כי קבלה ע"מ על מנת להשפיע נחשבת לצורת השפעה טהורה,(כמ"ש כמו שכתוב במסכת קדושין דף ז' באדם חשוב, נתנה היא ואמר הוא, הרי זו מקודשת, כי קבלתו שהיא ע"מ על מנת להנות לנותנת לו, נחשבת להשפעה ונתינה גמורה אליה, עש"ה עיין שם היטב), ואז קונה דבקות גמורה בו ית' יתברך כי דבקות הרוחני אינה אלא השואת הצורה, (כמ"ש כמו שאמרו חז"ל ואיך אפשר להדבק בו אלא הדבק במדותיו ע"ש עיין שם, מסכת שבת, דף קלג', ב') שבזה נעשה האדם ראוי לקבל כל הטוב והנועם והרוך שבמחשבת הבריאה.

לשם מה נברא כח שלילי בעולם?

יב) והנה נתבאר היטב דבר התיקון של הרצון לקבל המוטבע בנשמות מצד מחשבת הבריאה כי הכין הבורא ית' בשבילן ב' מערכות הנ"ל לעומת זה שעל ידיהן עוברות הנשמות ומתחלקות לב' בחינות, גוף ונפש, המתלבשים זה בזה, וע"י ועל ידי תורה ומצות, נמצאים בסופם, שיהפכו צורת הרצון לקבל כמו צורת הרצון להשפיע, ואז יכולים לקבל כל הטוב שבמחשבת הבריאה, ויחד עם זה זוכים לדבקות חזקה בו ית', מפאת שזכו ע"י העבודה בתורה ומצות, להשואת הצורה ליוצרם. שזה נבחן לגמר התיקון.

And then, there will be no need for the Impure Other Side, and it will be exterminated out of the earth and death will be swallowed up forever. And all the work in the Torah and the Precepts, which was given to all of humankind during the 6000 years of the existence of the world as well as to every individual during the 70 years of his life, is solely to bring them to complete the correction [of the souls and to arrive at] the said Similarity of Form.

And the subject of the coming into being and the emergence of the System of Impurity and of the *klipot* (shells) from the [Creator's] Holiness has also been thoroughly clarified. For this had to happen, in order to extend through it the creation of the bodies, which would later be corrected through the Torah and the Precepts. And if the bodies, with their damaging Desire to Receive, did not emerge [lit. extend] for us through the System of Impurity it would never have been possible for us to correct this desire because a person cannot correct something that he does not possess within him.

ואז, כיון שלא יהיה עוד שום צורך לס"א לסיטרא אחרא הטמאה, היא
תתבער מן הארץ ויבולע המות לנצח. וכל העבודה בתורה ומצות,
שניתנה לכלל העולם במשך שתא אלפי שני דהוי עלמא, וכן לכל
פרט במשך שבעים שנות חייו, אינה אלא להביאם לגמר התיקון של
השואת הצורה האמורה.

גם נתבאר היטב, ענין התהוות ויציאת מערכת הקליפות והטומאה
מקדושתו ית', שהיה מוכרח זה, כדי להמשיך על ידה בריאת
הגופים, שאח"כ שאחר כך יתקנו אותו ע"י על ידי תורה ומצות, ואם לא
היו נמשכים לנו הגופים ברצון לקבל שבהם המקולקל, ע"י על ידי
מערכת הטומאה, אז לא היה אפשר לנו לתקנו לעולם כי אין אדם
מתקן מה שאין בו.

Chapter Two: Free Will

How can we cleave and bond with non-physical essence?

13) Finally, there is yet one thing that we need to understand: After all, the Desire to Receive for the Self Alone is so flawed and damaging, how is it that it emerged in the Thought of Creation in the *Ein Sof* (Endless), Whose Unity is beyond any utterance and any word of explanation? The truth is indeed that His mere thought had completed and manifested everything instantly in the thought of creating the souls because He does not need an instrument of action as we do. And so instantly all the souls, as well as all the future worlds that were yet to be created, came out and came to be with all their ultimate and final perfection—with all the good and the pleasure and the pleasantness, that He thought for them, which the souls are destined to receive at the End of the *Tikkun* (Correction)—that is, after the Desire to Receive in the souls achieved complete correction, and it turned into pure bestowing in a complete Similarity of Form with the Emanator, Himself. This is because in His Eternity, the past and future and present serve as one; and the future serves Him like the present.

And the concept of lack of time does not apply to Him (*Zohar, Mishpatim* 51 and *Zohar Chadash, Beresheet* 243). And for this reason, the damaged Desire to Receive was not at all in a fragmented form in the *Ein Sof* (Endless); on the contrary, that Similarity of Form that is destined to be revealed in the future at the End of the *Tikkun* (Correction) emerged instantly in the Creator's Eternity. And on this secret, the sages said in *Pirkei* (the Chapters of) Rav Eliezer: Before the world was created, it was in a state of "He and His Name are One" because the separation form, which is in the Desire to Receive, had not yet been revealed in the existence of the souls that emerged in the Thought of Creation. Rather, [these souls] cleaved to Him in Similarity of Form, according to the secret of "He and His Name are One." And see the *Ten Luminous Emanations*, Branch A.

פרק שני: וזופש בוזירה

איך אפשר להדבק במשהו לא פיזי?

יג) אמנם עדיין נשאר לנו להבין, סוף סוף, כיון שהרצון לקבל לעצמו, הוא כל כך פגום ומקולקל, איך יצא והיה במחשבת הבריאה בא"ס ב"ה _{באין סוף ברוך הוא}, שלאחדותו אין הגה ומלה לפרשה. והענין הוא, כי באמת תכף במחשבה לברוא את הנשמות, היתה מחשבתו ית' גומרת הכל, כי אינו צריך לכלי מעשה כמונו, ותיכף יצאו ונתהוו, כל הנשמות וכל העולמות העתידים להבראות מלאים בכל הטוב והעונג והרוך שחשב בעדן, עם כל תכלית שלמותן הסופית, שהנשמות עתידות לקבל בגמר התיקון, דהיינו אחר שהרצון לקבל שבנשמות כבר קבל כל תיקונו בשלמות. ונתהפך להיות השפעה טהורה, בהשואת הצורה הגמורה, אל המאציל ית'. והוא מטעם כי בנצחיותו ית', העבר והעתיד וההוה משמשים כאחד, והעתיד משמש לו כהוה.

ואין ענין מחוסר זמן נוהג בו ית'. (זהר משפטים אות נ"א, ז"ח ברא' _{זוהר חדש, בראשית אות רמג}). ומטעם זה לא היה כל ענין הרצון לקבל המקולקל, בצורה דפרודא, בא"ס ב"ה _{באין סוף ברוך הוא}, אלא להיפך שאותה השואת הצורה, העתידה להגלות בגמר התיקון, הופיעה תיכף בנצחיותו ית'. ועל סוד הזה אמרו חז"ל (בפרקי דר"א _{בפרקי דרבי אליעזר}) קודם שנברא העולם היה הוא ושמו אחד כי הצורה דפרודא שברצון לקבל לא נתגלתה כלל במציאות הנשמות שיצאו במחשבת הבריאה, אלא הן היו דבוקות בו בהשואת הצורה, בסוד הוא ושמו אחד. וע"י בתע"ס _{ועיין בתלמוד עשר הספירות ענף א'}.

What are the three states of Creation?

14) You find out of necessity that generally there are three states to the souls. The first state is their existence in the *Ein Sof* (Endless) within the Thought of Creation, where they already have their future form that will appear at the End of the *Tikkun* (Correction). The second state is their existence over the 6000 years, where they were divided by the two above-mentioned Systems [of Impurity and Holiness] into body and soul, and were given the work with the Torah and the Precepts in order to transform the Desire to Receive in them into the Desire to Bestow Pleasure to their Maker, and not at all for themselves.

And during the period of this [second] state, no correction comes to the bodies, only to the *Nefesh* (Lower Soul). This means that they have to eradicate out of themselves any aspect of receiving for themselves, which is the aspect of the body, and remain only in the aspect of the Desire to Bestow, which is the form of the Desire of the soul. And even the souls of the *Tzadikim* (Righteous) will not be able to delight in paradise after death, only after their entire body has been decomposed in the earth.

The third state is the End of the *Tikkun* (Correction) of the souls after the Resurrection of the Dead; then the complete correction will reach the bodies as well, because then they will have transformed also the receiving itself, which is the form of the body, so that the form of pure bestowing will rest upon it, and they will be worthy of receiving for themselves all the goodness and delight and pleasure that exists in the Thought of Creation.

And with all this, they will gain the strong cleaving [to the Creator], by virtue of making their form similar to that of their Maker. Because they will not receive all this by virtue of their Desire to Receive, but rather by virtue of their Desire to Give Pleasure to their Maker, as He does enjoy when they receive from Him. And for the sake of brevity, I shall from now on use the names of these three states, namely the First State, the Second State and the Third State. And you shall remember all that has been explained here regarding each of these states.

מהם שלושת מצבי הבריאה?

יד) והנך מוצא בהכרח, שיש ג' מצבים לנשמות בדרך כלל. מצב הא' הוא מציאותן בא"ס ב"ה _{באין סוף ברוך הוא} במחשבת הבריאה, שכבר יש להן שם צורה העתידה של גמר התיקון. מצב ב', הוא מציאותן בבחינת שתא אלפי שני, שנתחלקו ע"י ב' _{על ידי} המערכות הנ"ל לגוף ונפש, וניתנה להן העבודה בתורה ומצות, כדי להפך את הרצון לקבל שבהן ולהביאו לבחינת רצון להשפיע נ"ר _{נחת רוח} ליוצרם, ולא לעצמם כלל.

ובמשך זמן מצב הזה, לא יגיע שום תיקון לגופים רק לנפשות בלבד, כלומר שצריכים לבער מקרבם כל בחינת הקבלה לעצמם שהיא בחינת הגוף, ולהשאר בבחינת רצון אך להשפיע בלבד. שזהו צורת הרצון שבנפשות. ואפילו נפשות הצדיקים לא תוכלנה להתענג בגן עדן אחר פטירתן, אלא אחר ככלות כל גופן להרקב בעפר.

מצב הג' הוא גמר התיקון של הנשמות אחר תחית המתים שאז יגיע התיקון השלם גם אל הגופין, כי אז יהפכו גם את הקבלה עצמה, שהיא צורת הגוף, שתתשרה עליה צורה של השפעה טהורה, ונעשים ראויים לקבל לעצמם כל הטוב והעונג והנועם שבמחשבת הבריאה.

ועם כל זה יזכו לדבקות החזקה, מכח השואת צורתם ליוצרם. כי לא יקבלו כל זה מצד רצונם לקבל, אלא מצד רצונם להשפיע נ"ר _{נחת רוח} ליוצרם, שהרי יש לו ית' הנאה שמקבלים ממנו. ולשם הקיצור אשתמש מכאן ואילך בשמות ג' המצבים הללו דהיינו מצב א' מצב ב' ומצב ג'. ואתה תזכור כל המתבאר כאן בכל מצב ומצב.

Is it "reward and punishment" or "cause and effect"?

15) And when you look at these three states, you will find that each one absolutely necessitates the existence of the other, to the extent that if it were possible for even a small part of any one of them to be cancelled, they all would be cancelled. For example, had the Third State, which is the transformation of the form of receiving to the form of bestowing not appeared then the First State, of necessity, could not have appeared in the *Ein Sof* (Endless). After all, the perfection emerged [in the First State] in its entirety only because [this perfection] was destined to become manifest in the Third State, which already served in His eternity as if it were in the present. And all the perfection that was shaped in there, in that state, was as if it had been copied from the future into the present that is there. So, had it been possible for the future to be cancelled, there would not have been any reality in the present.

Therefore, this means that the Third State requires all the reality of the First State. And even more so, if something is cancelled from the Second State—which is where we find all the work that is destined to be completed in the Third State, i.e., the work in correcting what is damaged, and in drawing down levels of souls—how will there ever be a Third State? So it follows that the Second State necessarily requires the Third State. Also, the existence of the First State in the Endless, where the perfection of the Third State is already present, absolutely requires it to match, that is to say, for the Second and the Third State to be revealed. That is, actually to [appear] with all the perfection that exists there, nothing less and nothing more.

So it follows that the First State itself requires, of necessity, that the systems should expand one opposite the other in the Second State of reality in order to enable [the manifestation of] a body with the Desire to Receive, which is damaged by the System of Impurity so that we can correct it. But had there not been a system of Worlds of Impurity, we would not have had this [flawed] Desire to Receive, and we could not have corrected it and reached the Third State because a person does not correct something that he does not

שכר ועונש או סיבה ותוצאה?

טו) וכשתסתכל בג' מצבים הללו, תמצא, שמחייבים זה את זה בהחלט גמור, באופן שאם היה אפשר שיתבטל משהו מאחד מהם, היו מתבטלים כולם. כי למשל אם לא היה מתגלה מצב הג', שהוא התהפכות צורת הקבלה לצורת השפעה, הרי בהכרח לא היה יכול לצאת מצב הא' שבא"ס ב"ה שבאין סוף ברוך הוא, שהרי לא יצאה שם כל השלמות, אלא מפני, שהעתיד להיות במצב הג' כבר שימש שם בנצחיותו ית' כמו הוה, וכל השלימות שנצטיירה שם באותו המצב, היא רק כמו העתקה מהעתיד לבא, אל ההוה אשר שם, אבל באם היה אפשר שיתבטל העתיד, לא היתה שם שום מציאות בהוה.

הרי שמצב הג' מחייב כל המציאות שבמצב הא'. ומכ"ש ומכל שכן בהתבטל משהו ממצב הב', ששם מציאות כל העבודה העתידה להגמר במצב הג', דהיינו העבודה בקלקול ותיקון, ובהמשכות מדרגות הנשמות, ואיך יהיה מצב הג'. הרי שמצב הב' מחייב את מצב הג', וכן מציאות מצב הא' שבא"ס ב"ה שבאין סוף ברוך הוא, שכבר נוהגת שם כל השלמות שבמצב הג', הרי הוא מחייב בהחלט שיותאם זה, דהיינו שיתגלה מצב הב' ומצב הג'. דהיינו ממש בכל אותה השלמות אשר שם, לא פחות משהו ולא יותר משהו.

הרי שמצב הא' עצמו מחייב בהכרח שתתפשטנה מערכות זו לעומת זו, במציאות הב', כדי לאפשר מציאות גוף ברצון לקבל המקולקל ע"י על ידי מערכת הטומאה, ואז אפשר לנו לתקנו. ואם לא היתה מערכת העולמות דטומאה, לא היה לנו הרצון לקבל הזה, ולא היה

possess within him. Therefore, we should not ask how the existence of the System of Impurity came about in the First State because, in fact, it is the First State that necessitates its reality [the reality of the System of Impurity] and its existence in the Second State.

Do we have free will?

16) We should not raise the question that, according to this, free will is annulled from us, Heaven forbid, because we have to achieve perfection and definitely get to the Third State, since it is already present in the First State. The point is that the Creator has prepared for us two ways in the Second State in order to bring us to the Third State. The first one is the Way of following the Torah and the Precepts in the manner that was clarified above.

The second is the Way of Suffering; where the suffering itself purifies the body and finally forces us to transform the Desire to Receive within us and to take the form of the Desire to Share and to thus cleave to the Creator. And this is according to what our sages said (in Tractate *Sanhedrin* 97b): "If you mend your ways, [then] good! And if not, I am installing over you a king like Haman, and against your will he will bring you back to the right path." And this is what our sages said about the scriptural passage: "…in its due time, I shall hasten it" —[that is,] if they have merit, I shall hasten it [the Final Redemption]; and if not, it will be in its due time (Tractate Sanhedrin, 98a).

The meaning here is that if we gain merit through the first way, which is by following the Torah and the Precepts, then we will hasten our *tikkun* (correction), and we will not need the hard and bitter suffering along with the sufficient length of time to get them [the suffering] so that they can return us to the right path against our will. And if not, [it will be] "in its due time," which means only after the period that the suffering will complete our correction, and the time of the correction is forced upon us against our will. The punishment of the souls in hell is also included in the way of suffering.

אפשר לתקנו ולבא למצב הג', כי אין אדם מתקן מה שאין בו. הרי שאין לשאול, איך נתהוותה ממצב הא' מערכת הטומאה, כי אדרבה מצב הא' הוא המחייב מציאותה ולהתקיים כן, במצב הב'.

האם יש לנו חופש בחירה?

טז) ואין להקשות לפי"ז א"כ אם כן לפי זה נתבטלה מאתנו הבחירה ח"ו חס ושלום, כיון שאנו מוכרחים להשתלם ולקבל המצב הג' בהחלט, מכח שכבר הוא מצוי במצב הא', והענין הוא, כי ב' דרכים הכין לנו השי"ת במצב הב', כדי להביאנו אל מצב הג'. הא' הוא, דרך קיום התורה ומצות, ע"ד על דרך שנתבאר לעיל.

ודרך הב' הוא, דרך יסורין, אשר היסורים בעצמם ממרקין את הגוף, ויכריחו אותנו לבסוף להפך את הרצון לקבל שבנו ולקבל צורת הרצון להשפיע, ולהדבק בו ית' יתברך. והוא ע"ד על דרך שאמרו חז"ל (סנהדרין צז, ע"ב) אם אתם חוזרים למוטב טוב, ואם לאו אני מעמיד עליכם מלך כהמן, ובעל כרחכם הוא יחזיר אתכם למוטב. וזה שאמרו [חכמינו] ז"ל על הכתוב, בעתה אחישנה, אם זכו אחישנה, ואם לא בעתה (סנהדרין, דף צח', א').

פירוש, אם זוכים על ידי דרך הא', שהוא ע"י קיום תורה ומצות, אז אנו ממהרים את התיקון שלנו, ואין אנו צריכים ליסורים קשים ומרים, ואריכות הזמן שיספיק לקבלם, שיחזירו אותנו למוטב בעל כרחנו. ואם לאו, בעתה, דהיינו רק בעת שהיסורים יגמרו את התיקון שלנו, ותגיע לנו עת התיקון בעל כרחנו. ובכלל דרך היסורים, הם גם עונשי הנשמות בגיהנם.

But one way or another, the End of the *Tikkun* (correction), which is the Third State, is absolutely required and guaranteed from the aspect of the First State, and the entire issue of our free will comes down to choose between the Way of Suffering and the Way of the Torah and the Precepts. Thus we have explained well how these three states of the soul are connected to each other and are required and essential for each other.

How can we fix something we do not possess?

17) From what has been explained, the said third inquiry that we have asked can be understood well. That is, when we look at ourselves we find ourselves being so damaged and despicable that there is no equal to us to be condemned, although when we look at the Maker Who created us, we should be so exquisitely lofty that there is no equal to us to be praised, as befits the Maker Who created us. This is because it is the nature of the Maker that is perfect, that His actions be perfect.

And from what has been said, it is well understood that this body of ours, with all its patterns and all its insignificant possessions, is not at all our real body. Our real body, namely, our eternal one, which is complete in every kind of perfection, already exists, placed and located in the Endless in the state of the First State, where it receives its complete form from what it is to be in the future in the Third State, i.e., Receiving in the form of Sharing, which is in Similarity of Form to the Endless.

And if indeed the First State itself dictates that we will, in the Second State, receive the *klipah* (shell) of this body of ours in its despicable and damaged form—that is, the Desire to Receive for the Self Alone, which is the force that creates the separation [of the soul] from the Endless, as we mentioned earlier—in order to correct it and to allow us to receive our eternal body in its complete form in the Third State, we should not protest angrily about that at all because our labor [of correction] would be possible only in this perishing and despicable body since a person cannot correct something that he does not possess within him.

אבל בין כך ובין כך, גמר התיקון שהוא מצב הג', הוא מחויב ומוחלט מצד המצב הא'. וכל הבחירה שלנו, היא רק בין דרך יסורין לבין תורה ומצות, והנה נתבאר היטב. איך ג' המצבים הללו של הנשמות קשורים זה בזה ומחייבים בהחלט זה את זה.

איך אפשר לתקן מה שאין בנו?

יז) ובהמתבאר מובנה היטב קושיא ג' הנ"ל שהקשינו, שבעת שאנו מסתכלים על עצמנו, אנו מוצאים את עצמנו מקולקלים ונבזים שאין כמונו לגנות, ובעת שאנו מסתכלים על הפועל שפעל אותנו, הרי אנו צריכים להיות ברום המעלות, שאין כמוהו לשבח, כיאות להפועל שברא אותנו. כי מטבע הפועל השלם שפעולותיו שלמות.

ובהאמור מובן היטב, שאותו הגוף שלנו בכל מקריו וקניניו האפסיים אינו כלל הגוף שלנו האמיתי, שהרי הגוף שלנו האמיתי, כלומר, הנצחי, השלם בכל מיני שלמות, כבר הוא מצוי עומד וקיים בא"ס ב"ה בא"ין סוף ברוך הוא בבחינת מצב הא', שמקבל שם צורתו השלמה מהעתיד להיות במצב הג', דהיינו קבלה בצורת השפעה, שהיא בהשואת הצורה לא"ס ב"ה אין-סוף ברוך הוא.

ואם אמנם מצבנו הא' עצמו מחייב שתנתן לנו במציאות הב' את הקליפה של אותו הגוף שלנו, בצורתה הבזויה והמקולקלת, שהוא הרצון לקבל אך לעצמו, שהוא כח הפירוד מא"ס ב"ה מא"ין-סוף ברוך הוא כן"ל, בכדי לתקנו, ולאפשר לנו לקבל הגוף הנצחי שלנו בפועל גמור במצב הג', אין לנו להתרעם על כך כלל, כי העבודה שלנו לא תצויר רק בגוף הזה הכלה ונפסד, כי אין אדם מתקן מה שאין בו.

Indeed, even in this Second State of ours, we truly are positioned in the same rate of perfection that is suitable and befits to the perfect Maker Who has created us because this body does not in any way cause us a defect. After all, this [Second State] body is destined to die and be canceled, and it is available for us only for the period of time necessary to cancel it so that we may receive our eternal form.

Why is there pain and suffering in the world?

18) At the same time, we are settling the fifth inquiry that we raised: How is it possible that from the Eternal will lead actions that are non-eternal and perishable? From what we have explained already, it is clear that truly we have emerged from within Him, as befits His Eternity, that is, as eternal beings in all perfection. And this eternity of ours dictates out of necessity that the shell of the body, which was given to us only for the labor [of correction], should be perishable and worthless because had it been eternal, Heaven forbid, we would have remained, Heaven forbid, eternally severed from the Essence of all life.

We have already said in verse 13 that this form of our body, which is the Desire to Receive for the Self Alone, does not exist at all in the eternal Thought of Creation because there we exist in our Third State form. But it [the form of our body] is completely necessary for us in the Second State of reality to enable us to correct it, as mentioned above. Nor should we ask at all regarding the condition of the rest of the created beings of the world, beside mankind, because mankind is the center of all Creation, as will be shown below (in verse 39). The other created beings do not count and have no value of their own, other than the extent that they help man to bring him to perfection, and therefore they rise and fall with him, without any significance on their own.

And together with this, we have clarified the fourth inquiry that we had raised: As it is the nature of the Good to act and do good [to others], how did the Creator create, from the beginning, creatures that would go through agony and suffering during their lifetimes?

באופן שבאמת אנו מצוים באותו שיעור השלמות הראוי ומותאם להפועל השלם שפעל אותנו במצבנו זה הב', כי זה אינו פוגם אותנו במשהו, שהרי הוא עומד למות ולהתבטל, ואינו מוכן לנו, רק בשיעור זמן, הנחוץ לבטלו, ולקבל צורתנו הנצחית.

מדוע יש סבל בעולם?

יח) ויחד עם זה, מיושבת קושיא ה' שהקשינו, איך אפשר שמנצחי תצאנה פעולות בלתי נצחיות הוות ונפסדות. ובהמתבאר מובן, כי באמת כבר יצאנו מלפנינו. כראוי לנצחיותו, דהיינו בריות נצחיות בכל השלמות, ונצחיותנו זו, מחייבת בהכרח, שקליפת הגוף הניתנה לנו רק לעבודה תהיה כלה ונפסדת, כי אם היתה נשארת בנצחיות ח"ו חס ושלום אז היינו נשארים נפרדים ח"ו חס ושלום מחי החיים לנצח.

וכבר אמרנו באות י"ג שצורה, זו של הגוף שלנו, שהוא הרצון לקבל אך לעצמו, אינה נמצאת כלל במחשבת הבריאה הנצחית, כי שם אנו עומדים בצורתנו של מצב הג'. אלא שהיא מחויבת לנו במציאות הב', כדי לאפשר לנו לתקנה כנ"ל. ואין לשאול כלל על מצב שאר בריות העולם, חוץ מהאדם, משום שהאדם הוא מרכז כל הבריאה, כמ"ש כמו שכתוב להלן (באות ל"ט) וכל שאר הבריות אין להן חשבון וערך של כולם לעצמן זולת באותו השיעור שהן מועילות לאדם להביאו לשלמותו, ועל כן הנה עולות ויורדות עמו, בלי שום חשבון לעצמן.

יט) ויחד עם זה מבוארת קושיא הד' שהקשינו, כיון שמדרך הטוב להיטיב, איך ברא מלכתחילה בריות שתתענינה ותתיסרנה במשך ימי חייהן כי כאמור, כל אלו היסורים מתחייבים ממצב הא' שלנו

As has been said, all this suffering is dictated by our First State, where our complete eternity that we receive from the future Third State forces us to take either the Way of the Torah or the Way of Suffering until we eventually reach our eternity in the Third State (as mentioned above in verse 15). And all this suffering pertains only to the shell of this body of ours, which was created only for death and burial. This teaches us that the Desire to Receive for the Self Alone in it [the body] was created only to be eradicated and erased from the world and to be transformed into the Desire to Share. Hence, the suffering that we undergo is nothing more than revelations to show us the insignificance [of the body] and the damage that is correlated to it.

Come and see, at the time when all the people in the world will agree unanimously to cancel and eradicate the Desire to Receive for the Self Alone that is in them, and they will have no other desire but to share with their fellow humans, then all the worries and malevolence will be eradicated from the world and everyone will have certainty about a healthy and wholesome life. This is because every one of us will then have the large world to take care of him and fulfill his needs. And indeed, at the time when everybody possesses only their Desire to Receive for the Self Alone, from this it develops into the source of all the worries and the suffering and the wars and the slaughter, which are inescapable, and which weaken our body with various sicknesses and afflictions.

And you will find that all the sufferings that exist in our world are only expressions brought about before our eyes to push us into canceling our evil bodily shell and receiving the wholesome form of the Desire to Share. And this is what we said, that the Way of Suffering is in itself capable of bringing us to the desired form. And you should know that the Precepts [concerning the relationship] between a person and his fellow humans takes priority over the Precepts between a person and the Creator because bestowing [goodness] upon a fellow human brings him to bestow [goodness] upon the Creator.

שנצחיותנו השלמה אשר שם המקובלת ממצב הג' העתיד לבא, מכריחה אותנו ללכת, או בדרך תורה או בדרך יסורין, ולבא ולהגיע לנצחיותנו שבמצב הג' (כנ"ל באות ט"ו) וכל אלו היסורין אינם שורים רק על קליפת הגוף שלנו הזו, שלא נבראה אלא למיתה וקבורה, שזה מלמד אותנו, שהרצון לקבל לעצמו שבו, לא נברא אלא רק למחותו ולהעבירו מהעולם, ולהפכו לרצון להשפיע. והיסורים שאנו סובלים, אינם אלא גילוים לגלות האפסיות וההזק הרובצת עליו.

ובוא וראה בעת שכל בני העולם יסכימו פה אחד, לבטל ולבער את הרצון לקבל לעצמם שבהם, ולא יהיה להם שום רצון אלא להשפיע לחבריהם, אז היו מתבטלים כל הדאגות וכל המזיקים מהארץ, וכל אחד היה בטוח בחיים בריאים ושלמים, שהרי כל אחד מאתנו, היה לו עולם גדול שידאג בעדו וימלא את צרכיו. אמנם בזמן שכל אחד אין לו אלא הרצון לקבל לעצמו, מכאן כל הדאגות היסורים והמלחמות והשחיטות, שאין לנו מפלט מהם, שהם מחלישים גופינו בכל מיני מחלות ומכאובים.

והנך מוצא, שכל אלו היסורים המצויים בעולמנו, אינם אלא גילוים מוצעים לעינינו, בכדי לדחוף אותנו לבטל את קליפת הגוף הרעה, ולקבל צורה השלמה של רצון להשפיע, והוא אשר אמרנו, שדרך היסורין בעצמו מסוגל להביאנו אל צורה הרצויה, ודע, שהמצות שבין אדם לחברו הן קודמות   למצוות שבין אדם למקום, כי ההשפעה לחברו מביאתהו להשפיע למקום.

Who am I? What am I?

20) Now that all this has been explained, the first inquiry that we raised: "What is our essence?" has been resolved. This is because our essence is the same as the essence of all the individuals in reality, which is nothing more and nothing less than the Desire to Receive (as mentioned above in verse 7). However, not as [this desire] appears to us now in the Second reality, which is the Desire to Receive for Itself Alone, but rather in the form that it exists in the First State, in the Endless, that is, in its eternal form, which is [the Desire] to Receive for the Sake of Giving pleasure to one's Maker (as mentioned above in verse 13).

And although we have not yet actually reached the Third State, and we still lack time still this does not blemish our core essence because our Third State is a necessity by virtue of the First State. Therefore, whatever is due to be collected is considered as already been collected and because we still lack time, it is considered a deficiency only when there is uncertainty as to whether we shall complete in this time what is needed to be completed. But since we do not have any doubt regarding this [in our ability to complete our correction], it is as if we have already reached the Third State. And the body in its negative form, that was given to us for now, [in the Second State] does not spoil our essence because it and all its properties will be eradicated together with the System of Impurity out of which they arose. And everything that is due to be burnt is already considered as if it is burnt, and is considered as if it had never existed.

Indeed, the *Nefesh* (Lower Soul), when by this body and whose essence is also an aspect of Desire, albeit a Desire to Share, which is extended to us from the system of the Four Worlds of *Atzilut* (Emanation), *Beriah* (Creation), *Yetzirah* (Formation), and *Asiyah* (Action) of Holiness (as mentioned above in verse 11), it [the *Nefesh*] exists for all eternity. This is because this form of the Desire

מי אני? מה אני?

כ) ואחר כל המתבאר, נפתרה לנו שאלה הא', ששאלנו, מה מהותנו. כי מהותנו היא כמהות כל הפרטים שבהמציאות, שהיא לא פחות ולא יותר מהרצון לקבל, (כנ"ל באות ז') אלא לא כפי שהוא מזדמן לנו עתה במציאות הב', שהוא הרצון לקבל אך לעצמו. אלא כפי שעומד וקיים במצב הא' בא"ס ב"ה באין סוף ברוך הוא, דהיינו בצורתו הנצחית, שהוא לקבל שהוא לקבל ע"מ על מנת להשפיע נ"ר נחת רוח ליוצרו, (כנ"ל באות י"ג).

ואע"פ ואף על פי שעוד לא הגענו בפועל למצב הג', ועדיין אנו מחוסרי זמן מכל מקום אין זה פוגם במשהו בעיקר מהותנו משום שמצבנו הג' מתחייב לנו בהחלט גמור מצד מצב הא' לפיכך כל העומד לגבות כגבוי דמי נחשב כאילו נגבה ומחוסר זמן, הנחשב לחסרון הוא רק במקום שיש ספק של משהו, אם ישלים את הצריך להשלים באותו זמן, וכיון שאין לנו שום ספק בזה, הרי זה דומה עלינו כמו שכבר באנו למצב הג', ואותו הגוף בצורתו הרעה הניתן לנו כעת, גם הוא אינו פוגם את מהותנו, להיותו הוא וכל קניניו עומדים להתבטל לגמרי יחד עם כל מערכת הטומאה שהיא מקורם, וכל העומד להשרף כשרוף דמי, ונחשב כמו שלא היה מעולם.

אמנם הנפש המלובשת בגוף ההוא שמהותה היא ג"כ גם כן בחינת רצון בלבד, אלא רצון להשפיע, שהיא נמשכת לנו ממערכת ד' העולמות אבי"ע אצילות, בריאה, יצירה, עשיה דקדושה, (כנ"ל באות י"א) היא קיימת לנצחיות, כי צורה זו של רצון להשפיע, הוא בהשואת

to Share is in Similarity of Form to Him, the Living Source of all Life and does not have any change within it, Heaven forbid. The elaboration of this matter will be explained below, from verse 32 onwards.

What are the three most common desires?

21) You should not let your heart sway after the opinions of the philosophers who claim that the very essence of the *Nefesh* (Lower Soul) is mental in nature [lit. substance]—that its being only comes to life through the intellectual thoughts it thinks, and from these it grows and makes up its whole being. And [they state further that] the subject of the continuation of the soul after the body dies depends entirely on the intellectual degree and knowledge that [the soul] has gained, to the point that if it has not gained this knowledge, then there is nothing by which the soul can continue to exist. [The philosophers] opinion is not that of the Torah and it also does not make sense (lit. is not acceptable to the heart). Any living being that has ever tried to gain intellectual knowledge knows and feels that this knowledge is [simply] something that is acquired and is not [itself] the essence of the one that acquires it.

But, as explained, all the substance of the renewed Creation, both the substance of the spiritual objects as well as the substance of the physical objects, is no more and no less than an aspect of the Desire to Receive (and even though we have said that the *Nefesh* (Lower Soul) is all about the Desire to Share). This [Desire to Share] comes only from the power of corrections of the Clothing of the Returning Light that it [the *Nefesh*] receives from the Higher Worlds, from whence it came to us[1]. The matter of this Clothing is explained well in *The Preface to the Wisdom of the Kabbalah* (verses 14, 15, 16,

---

1   i.e. the Desire to Share comes from the Higher World and is vested in the *Nefesh* and influences it, although the essence of the *Nefesh* is just the Desire to Receive.

הצורה לחי החיים, ואינה כלל ח"ו חס ושלום בת חילוף. ותשלום הענין
הוא להלן מאות ל"ב ואילך.

מהם שלושת סוגי הרצונות הנפוצים ביותר?

כא) ואל יסור לבך אחר דעת הפלוסופים האומרים, שעצם מהותה
של הנפש, היא חומר שכלי, והיותה באה רק מכח המושכלות
שמהן, שמהן מתגדלת והן כל הויתה, וענין השארת הנפש אחר
פטירת הגוף תלוי לגמרי בשיעור שכליות ומושכלות שקבלה, עד
שבהעדר לה המושכלות, אין כלל על מה שתחול השארת הנפש
אין זה דעת תורה. גם אינו מקובל כלל על הלב, וכל חי שניסה פעם
לקנות שכל, יודע ומרגיש שהשכל הוא קנין ואינו עצם הקונה.

אלא כמבואר, שכל חומר של הבריאה המחודשת, הן חומר של
העצמים הרוחניים והן חומר העצמים הגשמיים אינו לא פחות ולא
יותר מבחינת רצון לקבל (ואע"פ ואף על פי שאמרנו שהנפש היא כולה
רצון להשפיע). הוא רק מכח תיקונים של לבוש אור חוזר המקובל
לה מעולמות העליונים שמשם באה אלינו, שעניין לבוש הזה מבואר
היטב בפתיחה לחכמת הקבלה (באות יד טו, טז, יז, אמנם עצם
מהותה של הנפש היא ג"כ גם כן רצון לקבל ע"ש עיין שם ותבין זה)

and 19; indeed, the very essence of the *Nefesh* (Lower Soul) is also the Desire to Receive; study there and you will understand it). And all the perceptive ability that is given to us in order to distinguish between one object and another is distinguished only by [the different levels of] its Desire because the Desire that is in every being gives birth to his needs, and these needs breed thoughts and knowledge to the extent, that he will achieve and acquire those needs, because the Desire to Receive necessitates them.

And just as people's desires are different from each other, so, too, do their needs and their thoughts and their intellectual knowledge differ from each other. For example, [in the case of] the individuals whose Desire to Receive is limited only to animal lusts, then their needs and thoughts and intellectual knowledge would be solely to fulfill these desires in all their animal-like lust. And even though these people use their mind and intellectual knowledge like humans, in any case it is "like master like servant" [lit. enough for the slave to be like his master], and their mind is still like an Animal's mind because it is completely enslaved to and serves their Animal-like desires.

And with those whose Desire to Receive is especially strong with regard to human desires, such as honor and dominating others, [desires] which are not present in the Animal species, then the essence of all their needs and their thoughts and their learning is only to satisfy those desires to the fullest possible extent. And as for those whose Desire to Receive is invoked primarily in receiving intellectual education, then their main needs, thoughts, and learning are geared to satisfy this desire to its fullest.

וכל ההבחן הניתן לנו להבחין בין עצם לעצם, אינו נבחן משום זה, רק ברצונו בלבד, כי הרצון שבכל מהות, מוליד לו צרכים והצרכים מולידים לו מחשבות והשכלות בשיעור כזה, כדי להשיג את הצרכים ההם, אשר הרצון לקבל מחייב אותם.

וכשם שרצונות בני אדם שונים איש מרעהו, כן צרכיהם ומחשבותיהם והשכלתם שונים זה מזה, למשל, אותם שהרצון לקבל שבהם מוגבל בתאוות בהמיות בלבד, הרי צרכיהם ומחשבותיהם והשכלתם, רק בכדי למלאות הרצון הזה בכל מלואו הבהמי, ואע"פ ואף על פי שמשתמשים בשכל ודעת כאדם, מ"מ מכל מקום דיו לעבד להיות כרבו, והוא כשכל בהמי, להיות השכל משועבד ומשמש לרצון הבהמי.

ואותם שהרצון לקבל שלהם מתגבר בעיקר בתאוות אנושיות, כגון כבוד ושליטה על אחרים, שאינם מצוים במין הבהמה, הרי כל עיקר צרכיהם ומחשבותיהם והשכלותיהם רק בכדי למלאות להם הרצון ההוא בכל מלואו האפשרי. ואותם שהרצון לקבל שלהם מתגבר בעיקר לקבל מושכלות, הרי כל עיקר צרכיהם ומחשבותיהם והשכלותיהם למלאות להם הרצון הזה בכל מלואו.

Chapter Three: Resurrection of the Dead

Does energy disappear?

22) These three kinds of desires are present, for the most part, in all members of the human species, but they are blended in each individual differently [each one has all but the difference is in the priority and level of desire]. This is the foundation of the differences between one person and another. And from the material qualities we can also deduce regarding the properties of spiritual objects, according to their spiritual value.

23) In such a manner, [it is found] that even the *Nefesh* (Lower Soul) of the humans—which is spiritual and which, by virtue of the clothing by the Returning Light that they receive from the Higher Worlds whence they come from—have no desire other than to give pleasure to their Maker, and this Desire is the essence and the very being of the *Nefesh* (Lower Soul), as mentioned above [verse 21]. So, once [the *Nefesh*] is clothed with a human body, it [the *Nefesh*] gives birth in it [the body] to needs and thoughts and knowledge for the perpose of fulfilling [the *Nefesh*] own Desire to Share in the fullest possible manner. In other words, [the *Nefesh* wishes] to give pleasure to its Maker, according to the level of how much it desires.

24) And since the essence and very being of the body is the Desire to Receive for the Self Alone, and all of its interactions and its possessions are the fulfillment of this flawed Desire to Receive, which was created in the first place only to be exterminated and removed from the world in order [to allow the soul] to achieve the complete third state at the End of the *Tikkun* (Correction), therefore for this reason, it [the body] is a perishable and worthless mortal being, both itself and its possessions with it, like a passing shadow that does not leave a trace behind it.

And given that the essence and very being of the *Nefesh* (Lower Soul) is the Desire to Share, and all its interactions and possessions

פֶּרֶק שְׁלִישִׁי: תְּחִיַּת הַמֵּתִים

האם אנרגיה נעלמת?

כב) ואלו ג' מיני רצונות מצוים על פי רוב בכל מין האדם, אלא שמתמזגים בכל אחד בשיעורים אחרים. ומכאן כל השינוים שבין אדם לאדם. וממדות הגשמיות יש להקיש ג"כ ^{גם כן} למדות העצמים הרוחניים לפי ערכם הרוחני.

כג) באופן שגם נפשות בני אדם, הרוחניות, אשר מכח לבושי אור חוזר שמקבלות מעולמות העליונים שמשם באות, אין להן אלא רצון להשפיע נ"ר ^{נחת רוח} ליוצרן, שהרצון הזה הוא מהות ועצם הנפש, כנ"ל, נמצא אחר שמתלבשת בגוף האדם, היא מולידה בו צרכים ומחשבות והשכלות, למלאות הרצון להשפיע שלה בכל מלואו. דהיינו להשפיע נ"ר ^{נחת רוח} ליוצרה כפי מדת גדלו של הרצון שבה.

כד) ובהיות עצם ומהות הגוף רק רצון לקבל לעצמו, וכל מקריו וקנייניו הם מלואים של הרצון לקבל הזה המקולקל, שלא נברא מלכתחילה, אלא כדי לבערו ולכלותו מהעולם בכדי לבא למצב הג' השלם שבגמר התיקון, ע"כ ^{על כן} הוא בן תמותה כלה ונפסד, הוא וכל קנייניו עמו, כצל עובד שאינו מניח אחריו כלום.

ובהיות עצם ומהות של הנפש רק רצון להשפיע, וכל מקריה וקנייניה הם מלואים של הרצון להשפיע ההוא, שהוא כבר קיים ועומד במצב

are fulfillments of that Desire to Share, which already exists and is established in the eternal First State as well as in the Third State that is the future to come, therefore it [the soul] is not at all mortal and perishable, but it and all its possessions are eternal and alive and exist forever, and no fading or loss happens to them at all with the death of the body. In fact, the opposite is the case: The loss of the flawed and corrupt form of the body strengthens the soul considerably and allows it to ascend high at that time, towards Paradise.

And it has been well explained that the everlasting quality of the *Nefesh* (Lower Soul) does not depend at all on the knowledge that it has acquired, as those philosophers have claimed; rather, its eternal nature is in its very essence, that is, in the Desire to Share, which is its essence, while the knowledge that it has gained is its reward, not its essence.

What happens to the body through the *Tikkun* process?

25) From this, we have gained the full answer to our fifth inquiry, where we asked: Being that the body is so corrupted to the point that the *Nefesh* (Lower Soul) does not reach its ultimate sense of purity until the body has decomposed in the earth, why then does it [the body] return and stand up at the Resurrection of the Dead? And also what did our sages refer to when they said: "The dead shall resurrect with their faults, so they won't say he is another person!" (*Zohar, Sulam, Emor* verse 51 and *Kohelet Raba* 1:4) This issue you can understand well by referring to the Thought of Creation, namely the First State, because we said that since the Thought of Creation was to bestow pleasure upon His creatures, it is then necessary that He created an extremely big Desire to Receive all that great and good abundance included in the Thought of Creation, since the Great Pleasure and the Great Desire are one of the same (as mentioned above in sections 6 and 7, study this well).

We have said there that this great Desire to Receive is all the renewed substance that He has created because nothing more is required to

הא' הנצחי, וכן במצב הג' העתיד לבא, לפיכך אינה כלל בת תמותה
ובת חילוף, אלא היא וכל קנייניה עמה, המה נצחיים חיים וקיימים
לעד, ואין ההעדר פועל עליהם כלום בשעת מיתת הגוף, ואדרבה,
העדר צורת הגוף המקולקל, מחזק אותה ביותר ותוכל לעלות אז
למרומים לגן עדן.

ונתבאר היטב, שהשארת הנפש אינה תלויה כלל וכלל במושכלות
שקנתה, כדברי הפלוסופים הנ"ל, אלא נצחיותה היא בעצם מהותה
בלבד, דהיינו ברצון להשפיע שהוא מהותה. ועניין המושכלות
שקנתה הן שכרה, ולא עצמותה.

מה קורה לגוף בתהליך התיקון?

כה) ומכאן יצא לנו הפתרון המלא של חקירה ה', ששאלנו, כיון
שהגוף מקולקל כל כך עד שאין הנפש מצויה בכל טהרתה עד
שירקב הגוף בעפר, וא"כ ואם כן למה הוא חוזר ועומד לתחיית
המתים. וכן על מה שאמרו ז"ל, עתידים המתים להחיות במומם,
שלא יאמרו אחר הוא. (זהר אמור י"ז נ"א וכן מדרש קוהלת רבה, א', ד').
והעניין תבין היטב, ממחשבת הבריאה עצמה, דהיינו ממצב הא',
כי אמרנו, כיון שהמחשבה היתה להנות לנבראיו, הרי הכרח הוא,
שודאי ברא רצון גדול מופרז עד מאד. לקבל כל אותו השפע הטוב
שבמחשבת הבריאה. כי התענוג הגדול והרצון לקבל הגדול, עולים
בקנה אחד (כנ"ל באות ו' ז' עש"ה עיין שם היטב).

ואמרנו שם, שהרצון לקבל הגדול הזה, הוא כל חומר המחודש
שברא, מפני שאינו נצרך כלל ליותר מזה, כדי לקיים מחשבת

sustain the Thought of Creation. And it is the nature of the perfect Maker that He does not make anything superfluous, as it is said in *Shir HaYichud* (Song of Unification): "From all Your work, You have not forgotten and have not missed and have not favored one thing." And we have also said there that this excessive Desire to Receive was completely removed from the System of Holiness and was given to the system of the Worlds of Impurity, out of which the existence of bodies and their sustenance and all their possessions in This World emerges, until a person reaches the age of 13. It is through engaging with the Torah that he starts to attain the *Nefesh* (Lower Soul) of Holiness. Then he sustains himself from the system of the Worlds of Holiness, according to the level of greatness of the soul of Holiness that he has attained.

We also said above that during these 6000 years that have been given to us for engaging in the Torah and the Precepts, no corrections have come from it to the body that is the excessive Desire to Receive within it [the body], and all the corrections that come through our work reach the *Nefesh* (Lower Soul) only. [The *Nefesh*] ascends through [our spiritual work] to higher stages of holiness and purity, meaning to increase the Desire to Share that is extended together with the *Nefesh*. For this reason, the body is destined to die and be buried and rot because it has not received any of the corrections for itself.

Indeed, it [the body] cannot remain in this manner because after all, if the excessive Desire to Receive is removed from the world, then the Thought of Creation would not be fulfilled. Thought of Creation means that they will receive all the great pleasures that He intended to bestow upon His creatures. After all, the great Desire to Receive and the Great Pleasure are one of the same, and to the degree that the Desire to Receive is diminished, then the pleasure and enjoyment from the receiving are likewise [lit. to that extent] diminished.

הבריאה, ומטבע פועל השלם שאינו פועל דבר מיותר, כעין שאומר בשיר היחוד, מכל מלאכתך דבר אחד לא שכחת לא החסרת ולא העדפת. גם אמרנו שם, שהרצון לקבל המופרז הזה, הוסר לגמרי ממערכת הקדושה וניתן למערכת העולמות דטומאה, שממנה מציאות הגופים וכלכלתם וכל קניניהם בעולם הזה, עד שהאדם משיג י"ג שנה, שע"י על ידי עסק התורה מתחיל להשיג נפש דקדושה, שמתפרנס אז ממערכת העולמות דקדושה, לפי מדת גדלה של הנפש דקדושה שהשיג.

גם אמרנו לעיל, שבבמשך שתא אלפי שני, הניתנים לנו לעבודה בתורה ובמצות, אין שום תיקונים מגיעים מזה אל הגוף, דהיינו לרצון לקבל המופרז שבו, וכל התיקונים הבאים אז ע"י על ידי עבודתנו, הם מגיעים רק לנפש, שעולה על ידיהם במדרגות העליונות בקדושה וטהרה, שפירושו, רק להגדלת רצון להשפיע הנמשך עם הנפש, ומטעם זה סוף הגוף למות ולהקבר ולהרקב, כי לא קבל לעצמו שום תיקון.

אכן אי אפשר שישאר כך, כי סוף סוף, אם יאבד הרצון לקבל המופרז מהעולם, לא תתקיים ח"ו חס ושלום מחשבת הבריאה, דהיינו שיתקבלו כל התענוגים הגדולים אשר חשב להנות לנבראיו, שהרי הרצון   לקבל הגדול והתענוג הגדול, עולים בקנה אחד. ובשיעור שנתמעט הרצון לקבל, הרי בשיעור ההוא נפחתים התענוג וההנאה מן הקבלה.

For what purpose does the body have to come back to life?

26) We have already said that the First State absolutely necessitates the Third State, which emerged in its full extent from the Thought of Creation in the First State, without anything missing from it (as mentioned above in section 15). Therefore the First State necessitates the revival of the dead bodies, which is to say their excessive Desire to Receive, which had already perished and deteriorated and decomposed in the Second State, must be resurrected in all its excessive magnitude without any boundaries whatsoever, that is, with all its original defects.

Then the work starts anew in order to transform this excessive Desire to Receive so that it may be only to the degree in order to give [pleasure for the Creator], and then we will have gained two-fold: (1) We will have a space to receive all the goodness and pleasure and softness included in the Thought of Creation, by virtue of already having a body with an excessive Desire to Receive within it, which is completely in line with these pleasures, as mentioned above. (2) Since receiving in this manner will only be to the degree of giving pleasure to our Maker, then this receiving is considered completely bestowing (as mentioned above in section 11), we have also reached Similarity of Form, which is complete Cleaving [with the Creator] and which is our state in the Third State. Thus, the First State of necessity demands and necessitates the Resurrection of the Dead.

When will the Resurrection happen?

27) Indeed, it is not possible for there to be a Resurrection of the Dead except very close to the End of the *Tikkun* (Correction), that is, at the end of the Second [State of existence. Because after we have merited negating our excessive Desire to Receive and we have received the desire to only bestow, and after we have merited all the wondrous levels of the Soul, which are called *Nefesh* (Lower Soul), *Ruach* (Spirit), *Neshamah* (Soul), *Chayah* (Life-Sustaining) and

מדוע הגוף חייב לקום לתחיה?

כו) וכבר אמרנו שמצב הא', מחייב בהחלט את המצב הג', שיצא בכל השיעור המלא שבמחשבת הבריאה שבמצב הא', לא יחסר ממנו אף משהו (כנ"ל באות ט"ו), ולפיכך מחייב המצב הא' את תחיית הגופים המתים. כלומר, הרצון לקבל המופרז שלהם, שכבר כלה ונפסד ונרקב במציאות הב' מחייב לעמוד לתחייתו מחדש, בכל גודל שיעורו המופרז בלי מצרים כל שהם, דהיינו בכל המומים שהיו בו.

ואז מתחילה העבודה מחדש, בכדי להפוך הרצון לקבל המופרז הזה, שיהיה רק בשיעור כדי להשפיע, ואז הרוחנו פי שתים א) שיש לנו מקום לקבל כל הטוב והנועם והרוך שבמחשבת הבריאה, מכח שכבר יש לנו גוף המופרז מאד בהרצון לקבל שבו העולה בקנה אחד עם התענוגים הללו כנ"ל. ב) שמתוך שקבלנו באופן הזה, לא תהיה רק בשיעור להשפיע נחת רוח ליוצרנו, הרי קבלה זו כהשפעה גמורה נחשבת (כנ"ל באות י"א) ובאנו גם להשואת הצורה, שהיא הדבקות. שהיא צורתנו במצב הג'. הרי שמצב הא' מחייב את תחיית המתים בהחלט.

מתי תהיה תחיית המתים?

כז) אכן לא יתכן שתהיה תחית המתים, אלא קרוב לגמר התיקון, דהיינו בסופה של מציאות הב', כי אחר שזכינו לשלול את הרצון לקבל המופרז שלנו, וקבלנו את הרצון אך להשפיע, ואחר שזכינו לכל המדרגות הנפלאות שבנפש, המכונות נפש רוח נשמה חיה יחידה, ע"י על ידי עבודתנו בשלילת הרצון לקבל הזה, הנה אז, הרי

Yechidah (Oneness) by working on negating this Desire to Receive, we will then reach such great perfection that it is possible to bring the body back to life with the entirety of its excessive Desire to Receive. And, we are no longer harmed by [this desire] separating us from our Cleaving [with the Creator]; on the contrary, we overcome it, and we give it the form of [the Desire to] Bestow, as mentioned above.

Indeed, this is the way to conduct ourselves with every particular negative quality that we want to remove from ourselves: First, we have to completely remove it to its utmost reaches, so that nothing is left of it. Then, it is possible to go back and receive it and direct it in the way of equilibrium [lit. the middle path]. And as long as we have not completely removed it [the negative quality] from ourselves, we cannot in any way direct it according to the desired balanced way.

What will be the role of our body during the Resurrection?

28) This is what our sages meant when they said that the dead will be resurrected with all their defects (*Zohar, Sulam, Emor,* verse 51 and *Kohelet Raba* 1:4), and then afterwards they will be healed. This means, as we have said above, that at first the body shall be resurrected with its excessive Desire to Receive that has no boundary whatsoever. [This body] was raised under the chariot of the Worlds of Impurity before they had the merit of somehow purifying it [the body] even a little bit through the Torah and the Precepts. This is what is meant by "with all its defects." And then we start with the new work: to transform (lit. put) all this excessive Desire to Receive into Sharing [lit. form of bestowing], as was mentioned above; and that is when [the body] is healed because it has then achieved Similarity of Form [with its Maker].

And they [our sages] have said that the reason [for this resurrection of the flawed body] is so that no one would say he is someone else, meaning that it will not be said of him that he is in a different form

כבר באנו לשלמות הגדולה ביותר, עד שאפשר להחיות את הגוף
בחזרה, בכל הרצון המופרז שלו, ואין אנו נזוקים עוד ממנו
להפרידנו מדבקותנו, ואדרבה, אנו מתגברים עליו, ואנו נותנים לו
צורת השפעה, כנ"ל.

ובאמת כן הוא המנהג בכל מדה רעה פרטית, שאנו רוצים להעבירה
ממנו, שמתחילה אנו צריכים להסירה לגמרי עד קצה האחרון, שלא
ישאר ממנה כלום, ואח"כ ואחר כך אפשר לחזור ולקבלה ולהנהיגה
בדרך האמצעי. וכל עוד שלא הסרנו אותה כולה מאתנו. אי אפשר
כלל להנהיגה בדרך הרצוי הממוצע.

מה תפקיד הגוף בתחיית המתים ?

כח) וזה שאמרו חז"ל עתידים המתים להחיות במומם זוהר, הסולם,
אמור, סעיף נא', וכן מדרש קוהלת רבה, א', ד'), ואח"כ ואחר כך מתרפאים. דהיינו
כנ"ל, שמתחילה עומד לתחיה אותו הגוף, שהוא הרצון לקבל
המופרז בלי מצרים כל שהם, דהיינו כמו שנתגדל תחת מרכבת
העולמות הטומאה מטרם שזכו לטהרו במשהו ע"י על ידי תורה
ומצות, שזהו בכל מומו, ואז אנו מתחילים בעבודה חדשה, להכניס
כל הרצון לקבל המופרז הזה בצורת השפעה כנ"ל, ואז הוא נרפא,
כי עתה השיג גם השואת הצורה.

ואמרו הטעם, שהוא, שלא יאמרו אחר הוא, פירוש, שלא יאמרו
עליו, שהוא בצורה אחרת מהיותו במחשבת הבריאה, שהרי שם

than what he was in the Thought of Creation. After all, his excessive Desire to Receive stood there ready to receive all the goodness from the Thought of Creation, except that in the meantime, it was given to the *klipot* (shells) and it's possible to be purified. But, after all, it is not allowed to be a different body because if it will be missing any degree [of Desire], even a little bit, then it is as if it were entirely somebody else and [thus] will not at all be fit to [receive] all the goodness that is there in the Thought of Creation, in the same manner in which it would receive [all that goodness] in the First State. Understand this well.

עומד זה הרצון לקבל המופרז מכוון לקבלת כל הטוב שבמחשבת
הבריאה, אלא שבינתים ניתן אל הקליפות וניתן לטהרה, אבל סוף
כל סוף אסור שיהיה גוף אחר, שאם יהיה בשיעור פחות משהו,
הרי הוא כמו אחר לגמרי, ואינו ראוי כלל לכל הטוב שבמחשבת
הבריאה, כמו שכבר מקבל שם מבחינת מצב הא'. והבן היטב.

Chapter Four: I Desire, Therefore I am

Why is it important to develop and expand the desire for material things?

29) In all that has been explained so far, an opening has been created for us to settle the second question mentioned earlier, which is: During our short lifetime, what is our duty in the long chain of reality, of which we are very small links? You should know that our work during our lifetime of 70 years is divided into four divisions. In the first division, we attain the excessive Desire to Receive without boundaries, in all its flawed magnitude, under the control of the system of the Four Impure Worlds of: *Atzilut* (Emanation), *Beriah* (Creation), *Yetzirah* (Formation), and *Asiyah* (Action). This is because if we do not have this flawed Desire to Receive, we cannot correct it at all because nobody can correct something that they do not possess [See Chart A page 180].

Therefore, not only is this degree of Desire to Receive ingrained in the body in its source at its birth [lit. to the air of the world], it furthermore must be a vehicle for the impure *klipot* (Shells) for no less than 13 years. This means that the Shells must govern it and sustain it from their Lights [energy]. Their Lights keep increasing [the body's] Desire to Receive because the fulfillment of this Desire to Receive that the shells provide does nothing except constantly increase the demand of that Desire to Receive.

For example, at birth, [a person] has a desire for only one portion and no more; but when the *Sitra Achra* (Other Side) fulfills this desire for one portion, immediately the Desire to Receive grows and [the person] wants two hundred [portions]. And then, when the *Sitra Achra* provides him with the fulfillment of the two hundred [portions], the desire becomes [even] larger and he wants four hundred [portions]. And if [this person] does not overcome himself through the Torah and the Precepts to purify the Desire to Receive and to turn it into [the Desire to] Bestow, then his Desire to Receive will keep getting larger throughout his life, to the point that "there is not one person who dies having [even] half of his desires fulfilled."

פרק רביעי: אני רוצה - משמע אני קיים

מדוע חשוב לפתח ולהגדיל את הרצון לקבל הגשמי של הגוף?

כט) ובכל המתבאר נפתח לנו הפתח ליישב שאלה הב' הנ"ל, דהיינו מה תפקידנו בשלשלת המציאות הארוכה, שאנו טבעות קטנות הימנה, במשך ימי שני חיינו הקצרים. ותדע, שעבודתנו במשך ע' [70] שנותינו מתחלקת לד' חלוקות: חלוקה א) הוא להשיג את הרצון לקבל המופרז בלי מצרים, בכל שיעורו המקולקל, מתחת יד מערכת ד' העולמות אבי"ע אצילות, בריאה, יצירה, עשיה הטמאים. כי אם לא יהיה בנו הרצון לקבל המקולקל הזה, לא נוכל כלל לתקנו, כי אין לך מי שיתקן דבר שאין בו [ראו טבלה א' עמוד 181].

ולפיכך, לא די אותו שיעור הרצון לקבל, המוטבע בגוף ממקור לידתו לאויר העולם, אלא עוד, שמוכרח להיות מרכבה לקליפות הטמאות לא פחות מי"ג שנים, כלומר שהקליפות תהינה שולטות עליו, ותתנה לו מאורותיהן, שהאורות שלהן הולכים ומגדילים את הרצון לקבל שלו, כי המלואים שהקליפות מספיקות אל הרצון לקבל, אינם אלא מרחיבים והולכים את התביעה של הרצון לקבל.

למשל כשנולד אין לו תאוה אלא למנה, ולא יותר, אבל כשהס"א הסטרא אחרא, הצד האחר ממלאת לו המנה, תכף נרחב הרצון לקבל, והוא רוצה מאתים, ואח"כ כשנותנת לו הס"א הסטרא אחרא, הצד האחר את המלוי מאתים, מיד נרחב הרצון ורוצה ד' מאות, ואם אינו מתגבר על ידי תורה ומצות לטהר את הרצון לקבל ולהפכו להשפעה, הרי הרצון לקבל שלו הולך ומתרחב במשך שנות חייו, עד שאין אדם מת וחצי תאותו בידו.

And this is considered that he is under the dominion of the *Sitra Achra* (Other Side) and of the *klipot* (Shells), whose purpose is to expand and enlarge his Desire to Receive and to make it excessive and without any boundary whatsoever. The reason for this is to provide that person with all the substance that he needs to work on it and correct it.

Why is it important to develop and expand the spiritual Desire to Receive of the soul?

30) The second division [in a person's lifetime] is from the age of 13 onwards, during which strength is given to that Point in his Heart, which is the secret of the Back of the *Nefesh* (Lower Soul) of Holiness, which is clothed with his Desire to Receive from the moment of his birth, although it [that Point in his Heart] does not start waking up until the age of 13 years (for the said reason). And then he starts to fall under the dominion of the system of the Worlds of Holiness, according to the degree that he engages with Torah and the Precepts. And his main purpose at this time is to achieve and enlarge his spiritual Desire to Receive because from the moment of his birth, he has had no Desire to Receive except for physicality [see Chart A page 180].

Therefore, even though he has attained the excessive Desire to Receive before 13 years of age, this is not the end of the growth of his Desire to Receive. The core growth of this Desire to Receive can only be achieved in spirituality. For example, before the age of 13, his Desire to Receive craved swallowing all the riches and the honor of this material world, and it is evident to all that for him, it is a world that is not eternal and that is available to everyone only as a fleeting shadow, that is here one moment and gone the next. This is not the case when he acquires the excessive spiritual Desire to Receive because then he wants to swallow for his own enjoyment all the goodness and the riches of the eternal World to Come, which for him is an acquisition of eternity and immortality. Thus, the essence of the excessive Desire to Receive is not completed unless it is a Desire to Receive spirituality.

וזה נבחן שהוא מצוי ברשות הס"א הסטרא אחרא, הצד האחר והקליפות, שתפקידן להרחיב ולהגדיל את הרצון לקבל שלו ולעשותו מופרז בלי מצרים כל שהם. דהיינו בכדי להמציא להאדם כל החומר שהוא צריך לעבוד בו ולתקנו.

מדוע חשוב לפתח ולהגדיל את הרצון לקבל הרוחני של הנשמה?

ל) חלוקה ב) הוא מי"ג שנים ואילך, שאז ניתן כח לנקודה שבלב שבו, שה"ס שהוא סוד אחורים של הנפש דקדושה, המלובשת בהרצון לקבל שלו, מעת לידתו, אלא שאינה מתחלת להתעורר רק אחר י"ג שנים (שהוא מטעם הנ"ל) ואז הוא מתחיל להכנס תחת רשות מערכת העולמות דקדושה, דהיינו בשיעור שהוא עוסק בתורה ומצות. ועיקר התפקיד בעת ההיא, הוא להשיג ולהגדיל את הרצון לקבל הרוחני. כי מעת לידתו אין לו רצון לקבל אלא לגשמיות בלבד [ראו טבלה א' עמוד 181].

ולפיכך אע"פ ואף על פי שהשיג הרצון לקבל המופרז מטרם י"ג שנים, אינו עוד גמר גדלותו של הרצון לקבל, ועיקר גדלות הרצון לקבל, מצוירת רק ברוחניות כי למשל מטרם י"ג שנים חשק הרצון לקבל שלו לבלוע כל העושר והכבוד שבעוה"ז העולם הזה הגשמי, אשר גלוי לכל, שהוא בעדו, עולם שאינו נצחי, המצוי לכל אחד רק כצל עובר חלף ואינו. משא"כ מה שאין כן כשמשיג הרצון לקבל המופרז הרוחני, הרי אז הוא רוצה לבלוע להנאתו כל הטוב והעושר שבעוה"ב בעולם הבא הנצחי, שהוא בעדו קנין עדי עד ולנצחיות. הרי שעיקר הרצון לקבל המופרז אינו נגמר, אלא ברצון לקבל רוחניות.

Can we fall in love with the Creator?

31) And this is what has been referred to in the *Tikkunim* (*Zohar New Corrections* 97:b) about the scriptural passage: "The Leech has two daughters; '*Hav, Hav* (give, give) they cry." (Proverbs 30:15) "Leech" here refers to *Gehinnom* (Hell), and the wicked who are trapped in this Hell cry out like a dog: "*Hav, Hav*" (give, give), that is to say, "Give us the riches of This World; give us the riches of the World to Come."

And yet, in spite of all this, it [the excessive Desire to Receive] is an immeasurably more important stage than the first one because besides possessing the real magnitude of the Desire to Receive and being provided with all the 'substance' that [a person] needs for the [spiritual] work, it is this stage that leads him to [be busy with the Torah] For its own Sake, as our sages said (in Tractate *Peshachim* 50:b): A person should always engage with the Torah and the Precepts [even] Not For its own Sake, because out of Not For its own Sake [a person] comes to For its own Sake.

For this reason, the following stage, which comes after 13 years of age, is considered to be an aspect of Holiness, and this is the secret of the "maidservant of Holiness who is serving her mistress," who is the secret of the Holy *Shechinah* (Divine Presence). It is the maidservant who brings him to For its own Sake, and so he merits the presence of the Shechinah. Still, he has to apply all the appropriate means in order to come to For its own Sake, because if he does not make that effort and, Heaven forbid, does not come to For its own Sake, then he falls into the trap of the Maidservant of Impurity, who is opposite to the Maidservant of Holiness and whose whole focus is to confuse the human being, so that engaging Not For its own Sake would not lead him to For its own Sake. And on her [that is, the Maidservant of Impurity] it has been said: "a Maidservant that succeeds her mistress" (Proverbs 30:23) because she does not let the human being come close to the mistress, which is the Holy *Shechinah* (Divine Presence).

האם אפשר להתאהב בבורא?

לא) וז"ש וזה שכתוב בתקונים (תקונים חדשים צ"ז ע"ב) על הכתוב
לעלוקה שתי בנות הב הב (משלי ל') שעלוקה פירושו גיהנם,
והרשעים הנלכדים בגיהנם זה, צווחין ככלבא הב הב דהיינו הב לן
עותרא דעלמא הדין, הב לן עותרא דעלמא דאתי תן לנו את העושר של
העולם הזה ותן לנו את העושר של העולם הבא.

ועם כל זה הוא מדרגה חשובה לאין ערך יותר מראשונה, כי מלבד
שמשיג שיעור הגדלות האמיתית של הרצון לקבל, וניתן לו לעבודה
כל החומר כולו שהוא צריך, הנה היא המדרגה המביאתו לשמה,
כמו שאמרו חז"ל (פסחים נ' ע"ב) לעולם יעסוק אדם בתורה ומצות
[אפילו] שלא לשמה, שמתוך שלא לשמה בא לשמה.

וע"כ על כן נבחנת המדרגה הזו הבאה לאחר י"ג שנה לבחינת קדושה,
וה"ס הוא סוד השפחה דקדושה המשמשת לגבירתה. שה"ס שהוא סוד
השכינה הקדושה. כי השפחה מביאתו לשמה, וזוכה להשראת
השכינה. אמנם הוא צריך לעשות כל האמצעים המותאמים שיבא
לשמה, כי אם לא יתאמץ לזה, ולא יבא ח"ו חס ושלום לשמה, הרי
הוא נופל בפח השפחה הטמאה, שהיא הלעומת דשפחה דקדושה,
שענינה לבלבל את האדם, שהלא לשמה לא יביאהו לשמה. ועליה
נאמר, ושפחה כי תירש גבירתה (משלי ל'), כי לא תניחהו לאדם
להתקרב אל הגבירה שהיא השכינה הקדושה.

And the final stage in this division is that [a person] falls in love with the Creator with great passion, similar to a passionate person who is so inflamed with material lust to the degree that this lust does not leave him all day and all night. In the words of the poet: "When I remember it, it does not let me sleep." And it is also said about him: "Lust is aroused by the Tree of Life." (Proverbs 13:12) This is so because the five levels of the soul are the secret of the Tree of Life, whose span is 500 years, as each level is 100 years. This means that it will lead him to obtain all these levels [of the soul]: *Nefesh* (Lower Sustaining), *Ruach* (Spirit), *Neshamah* (Soul), *Chayah* (Life-Sustaining), and *Yechidah* (Oneness), which are explained in the third division.

What will be our role after the Resurrection of the Dead?

32) The third division is the [spiritual] work with the Torah and the Precepts For its own Sake, which means in order to bestow, in order not to receive a reward [See Chart A page 180]. This work purifies [the person's] Desire to Receive for the Self Alone and turns it into a Desire to Share, which, to the level of purity of the Desire to Receive, makes him worthy and prepared to receive the five parts of the soul, which are called *Nefesh* (Lower Soul), *Ruach* (Spirit), *Neshamah* (Soul), *Chayah* (Life-Sustaining), and *Yechidah* (Oneness) [Chart #1].

CHART #1

The five parts of the soul

Yechidah (Oneness)
Chayah (Life-Sustaining)
Neshamah (Soul)
Ruach (Spirit)
Nefesh (Lower Soul)

והמדרגה הסופית שבחלוקה זו, היא שיתאהב בהקב"ה בתאוה גדולה, בדומה לבעל תאוה המתאהב בתאוה גשמית עד שאין התאוה סרה מנגד עיניו כל היום וכל הלילה, וע"ד עלדרך שאמר הפיטן בזכרי בו אינו מניח לי לישון. ואז נאמר עליו, ועץ חיים, תאוה באה (משלי י"ג) כי ה' מדרגות הנשמה ה"ס הוא סוד עץ החיים, שמהלכו חמש מאות שנה. שכל מדרגה היא בת מאה. דהיינו כי יביאהו לקבל כל אלו ה' בחינות נרנח"י נפש רוח נשמה חיה יחידה המבוארות בחלוקה הג'.

מה יהיה תפקידנו אחרי תחיית המתים?

לב) חלוקה ג) הוא העבודה בתורה ומצות לשמה, דהיינו על מנת להשפיע, ושלא לקבל פרס [ראו טבלה א' עמוד 180]. שעבודה זו מטהרת את הרצון לקבל לעצמו שבו, ומהפכתו ברצון להשפיע, אשר בשיעורי הטהרה של הרצון לקבל, נעשה ראוי ומוכשר לקבל ה' חלקי הנפש הנקראות נרנח"י נפש רוח נשמה חיה יחידה (להלן באות מ"ב) [טבלה 1#].

טבלה 1#

חמשת חלקי הנשמה

יחידה
חיה
נשמה
רוח
נפש

This is because they are structured as the Desire to Share (as mentioned above in section 23) and cannot enter and be clothed with its body as long as the Desire to Receive, which is in opposite form to the soul, or even in Difference of Form, dominates him. This is because the matter of covering (lit. vestments) oneself and the Similarity of Form are aligned with each other (as discussed earlier in section 11).

And once the person merits to be completely with the Desire to Share and not for his own sake at all, this indicates that he has merited Similarity of Form to his own supernal *Nefesh* (Lower Soul), *Ruach* (Spirit), *Neshamah* (Soul), *Chayah* (Life-Sustaining), and *Yechidah* (Oneness) -- which are extended from the first stage from their source in the *Ein Sof* (Endless) through the [Worlds of] *Atzilut* (Emanation), *Beriah* (Creation), *Yetzirah* (Formation), and *Asiyah* (Action) of Holiness -- and they will immediately be drawn to him and enclothe themselves with him gradually.

The fourth division is the work that is applied after the Resurrection of the Dead, that is, when the Desire to Receive, after it has been completely absent through death and burial, returns and is again alive with the worst form of excessive Desire to Receive. This is the secret meaning of the saying that the dead are destined to be resurrected with their defects (as mentioned above in section 28). And then they transform it [the body] into Receiving in the form of Sharing, as was explained there at length. Indeed, there are some uniquely selected individuals who are given this work while still alive in This World [See Chart A, page 180].

כי הן עומדות ברצון להשפיע (כנ"ל באות כ"ג) ולא תוכלנה
להתלבש בגופו, כל עוד שהרצון לקבל שולט בו, הנמצא עם הנפש
בהפכיות הצורה, או אפילו בשינוי צורה, כי ענין התלבשות, והשואת
הצורה, עולות בקנה אחד (כנ"ל באות י"א).

ובעת שיזכה שיהיה כולו ברצון להשפיע ולא לצורך עצמו כלום,
נמצא שזכה בהשואת הצורה לנרנח"י נפש רוח נשמה חיה יחידה שלו
העליונים, (שהן נמשכות ממקורן בא"ס ב"ה באין סוף ברוך הוא ממצב
הא' דרך אבי"ע אצילות, בריאה, יצירה, עשיה דקדושה) ותכף תמשכנה
אליו ותתלבשנה בו, בדרך המדרגה.

חלוקה ד) הוא העבודה הנוהגת אחר תחית המתים, דהיינו שהרצון
לקבל, אחר שכבר נעדר לגמרי ע"י מיתה וקבורה, עומד שוב
לתחיה לקבל המופרז הגרוע ביותר, שה"ס שהוא סוד עתידים
המתים להחיות במומם (כנ"ל באות כ"ח) ואז מהפכים אותו על
קבלה בצורת השפעה, כמ"ש כמו שכתוב שם באורך. אמנם יש יחידי
סגולה שניתנה להם עבודה זו גם בחיים חיותם בעוה"ז העולם הזה
[ראו טבלה א', עמוד 181].

Chapter Five: Will Power

Really??... Was this whole world created just for me?

33) The sixth inquiry has remained for us to explain, regarding what the sages told us: that all the Upper and Lower Worlds were created solely for the sake of the human being (lit. man) (Tractate Sanhedrin, 37). It seems very puzzling that the Creator would bother to create all these worlds for this puny man, who is not even a thin hair in comparison with all reality that we see here in This World, and how much less so when compared to the Supernal Spiritual Worlds. And even more puzzling [is the question]: What need does a man have for all these multiple great spiritual worlds?

It is important that you know that all the pleasure of our Creator in bestowing fulfillment to His created beings is proportionate to the degree that those beings feel that He is the One Who bestows and Who gives them joy because then He has great enjoyment with them. As a father who plays with his beloved son, to the extent that the son feels and recognizes the greatness and loftiness of his father, and the father shows him all the treasures that he has prepared for him, as the Scriptures say: "My dearest son, Ephraim! For is he not my darling child? For as often as I speak about him, I do remember him still. Therefore my heart yearns for him; I will surely have mercy on him, says the Creator." (Jeremiah 31:20)

Examine this text well and you could educate yourself and know the great enjoyment that the Creator derives from those who have reached perfection and who have merited feeling Him and recognizing His greatness in all the various ways that He has prepared for them, until He appears to them as a father relating to his beloved son, as a father with his playful son, etc. All this appears in the text for the eyes of the educated ones. But we should not speak at length about things of this nature because it is enough for us to know that for the sake of His pleasure and enjoyment with those perfected ones, it was worth it for Him to create all the Worlds, both the Upper and Lower ones, as will be made clear below.

פרק וזמישי: כוח רצון

באמת?? כל העולם נברא בשבילי?

לג) ועתה נשארה לנו לבאר חקירה הו', מ"ש מה שאמרו חז"ל שכל העולמות העליונים ותחתונים לא נבראו אלא בשביל האדם (מסכת סנהדרין, עמוד לז'), שלכאורה תמוה מאוד, שבשביל אדם הקטן, שאינו אפילו בערך דקה שערה כלפי המציאות שלפנינו בעוה"ז העולם הזה, ומכ"ש ומכל שכן כלפי העולמות העליונים הרוחניים, יטרח הבורא ית' יתברך לברוא כל אלו בשבילו. ועוד יותר תמוה, למה לו לאדם כל אלו העולמות הרוחניים האדירים המרובים.

וצריך שתדע, שכל נחת רוח של יוצרנו ית' להנות לנבראיו, היא במדה שהנבראים ירגישו אותו ית', שהוא המשפיע, והוא המהנה אותם, אשר אז יש לו שעשועים גדולים עמהם, כאב המשתעשע עם בנו החביב לו, בה במדה שהבן מרגיש ומכיר גדולתו ורוממותו של אביו, ואביו מראה לו כל האוצרות שהכין בשבילו. כמו שאומר הכתוב (ירמיה ל"א) הבן יקיר לי אפרים, אם ילד שעשועים, כי מדי דברי בו זכור אזכרנו עוד, על כן המו מעי לו, רחם ארחמנו נאום ה'.

והסתכל היטב בכתוב הזה ותוכל להשכיל ולדעת את השעשועים הגדולים של השי"ת עם אותם השלמים, שזכו להרגישו ולהכיר גדולתו בכל אותם הדרכים שהכין בעדם, עד שיבא עמהם ביחס של אב ובנו היקר, כאב עם ילד שעשועים שלו, וכו', ככל המבואר בכתוב לעיני המשכילים. ואין להאריך בכגון זה. כי די לנו לדעת, אשר בשביל הנ"ר נחת רוח והשעשועים האלו עם השלמים הללו, היה כדאי לו לברוא את כל העולמות, העליונים ותחתונים יחד, כמו שיתבאר לפנינו.

71

34) To prepare His created beings so that they could reach the lofty and exalted stage mentioned above, the Creator wanted to accomplish this through a sequence of four stages, which evolve one out of the other and are referred to as Inanimate, Vegetative, Animal, and Speaking (Human). And these are really the four phases of the Desire to Receive by which each and every world of the Supernal Worlds is divided into. Although the main objective lies in the fourth phase of the Desire to Receive, it is still not possible for this fourth phase to be revealed at once. Rather, [it has to happen] through the power of the three phases that come before it, and it is revealed and develops in them and through them gradually [lit. slowly] until it has been completed in all its form in the fourth phase, as it is explained in the *Ten Luminous Emanations* (Study of the Ten *Sefirot*), Part 1, paragraph 50, beginning with the words: "And the reason…"

What are the four stages of the Desire to Receive?

35) In the first phase of the Desire to Receive, which is called Inanimate and which begins to reveal the Desire to Receive in this physical world, there is simply a collective force of motion to all of the Inanimate species; however, in the individual segments of it no movement can be discerned with the naked eye. This is because the Desire to Receive gives birth to needs and the needs give birth to sufficient movements in order to achieve and get those needs. And because the Desire to Receive is limited to a small quantity, it governs only the entire collective [of Inanimate world] at once, and its dominion over individual details cannot be discerned [See Chart B, page 182].

36) To this, [the aspect of] the Vegetative is added, and they are the second phase of the Desire to Receive, whose degree [of Desire] is greater than its degree [of the Desire] in the Inanimate. Here the Desire to Receive governs each and every individual of all its partitions. This is because every part has its own individual movement, which allows it to expand lengthwise and widthwise, and moves in the direction of the sunrise. Also, one can discern

לד) ובכדי להכין את בריותיו, שתוכלנה להגיע למדרגה הרמה
והנשאה הנזכרת, רצה הקב"ה לפעול זה על סדר ד' מדרגות,
המתפתחות אחת מחברתה, הנקראות דומם צומח חי מדבר. והן
באמת ד' בחינות של הרצון לקבל, שכל עולם ועולם מעולמות
עליונים מתחלק בהן. כי אע"פ על פי אף שעיקר החפץ הוא בבחי"ד
בבחינה ד' של הרצון לקבל, אמנם אי אפשר שתתגלה בחי"ד בבחינה
ד' בבת אחת, אלא בכח ג' בחינות הקודמות לה, שהיא מתגלית
ומתפתחת בהן ועל ידיהן לאט לאט עד שנשלמה בכל צורתה
שבבחי"ד בבחינה ד'. כמבואר בתע"ס תלמוד עשר הספירות חלק א' אות נ' ד"ה
דבור המתחיל [במילה] וטעם.

מהן ארבע הדרגות של הרצון?

לה) והנה בחי"א בחינה א' של הרצון לקבל הנקרא דומם, שהיא
תחילת גילוי של הרצון לקבל בעוה"ז העולם הזה הגשמי, אין שם
אלא כח תנועה כולל לכל מין הדומם, אבל בפרטים שלו אינה ניכרת
לעין שום תנועה. כי הרצון לקבל מוליד צרכים והצרכים מולידים
תנועות מספיקות עד כדי להשיג את הצורך. וכיון שהרצון לקבל
הוא במדה מועטת, אינו שולט רק על הכלל כולו בבת אחת, ואינה
ניכרת שליטתו על הפרטים [ראו טבלה ב', עמוד 183].

לו) נוסף עליו הצומח, שהוא בחי"ב בחינה ב' של הרצון לקבל, שמדתו
כבר גדולה יותר ממדתו שבדומם, והרצון לקבל שבו שולט בכל
פרט ופרט מהפרטים שלו. כי כל פרט יש לו תנועה פרטית לעצמו,
שמתפשט לארכו ולרחבו, ומתנועע למקום זריחת השמש, וכן ניכר
בהם, ענין של אכילה ושתיה והוצאת הפסולת, לכל פרט ופרט.

in each and every part the matter of "eating" and "drinking" and "elimination of waste." But with all this, they do not have yet free individual emotion in each and every part [See Chart B, page 182].

37) To this [the aspect of] the Animal species is added. This is the third phase of the Desire to Receive, and its degree has been completed to a greater extent, for this Desire to Receive already gives birth to free and individual emotions in each part, which is [in effect] the unique life in each part in a different manner from the other. At the same time, they still do not have any feeling for each other; in other words, they have no preparation to be sorry in the sorrow of their fellow friend or be happy in the happiness of their fellow friend, etc[See Chart B, page 182] .

38) Added to all these is [the aspect of] the Human species, which is the fourth phase of the Desire to Receive, which is now in its complete and final degree [of the Desire to Receive]. This is because, both the Desire to Receive as well as a feeling for the other are active in him. And if you want to know with great accuracy what the difference is between the third phase of the Desire to Receive, which is in the Animal species, and the fourth phase of the Desire to Receive, which can be found in Human species, I can tell you that it is like the difference between the value of one individual of the reality as compared to the entire reality [Chart #2].

CHART #2

Levels of Desire to Receive

Levels	Desire	Phase
Inanimate	Small	First
Vegetative	Big	Second
Animal	Bigger	Third
Speaking	Biggest (Endless)	Fourth

ועכ"ז ועם כל זה עוד לא נמצא בהם הרגש חפשי פרטי לכל אחד [ראו טבלה ב', עמוד 183].

לז) נוסף עליו מין החי, שהוא בחי"ג בחינה ג' של הרצון לקבל, ומדתו כבר נשלמה במדה מרובה, שהרצון לקבל הזה כבר מוליד בכל פרט ופרט הרגש חפשי פרטי, שהוא החיים המיוחדים לכל פרט באופן משונה מחברו. אמנם עדיין אין בהם הרגש זולתו, והיינו שאין בהם שום הכנה. להצטער בצרת חברו או לשמוח בשמחת חברו, וכדומה [ראו טבלה ב', עמוד 183].

לח) נוסף על כולם מין האדם, שהוא בחי"ד בחינה ד' של הרצון לקבל, והוא כבר במדתו השלמה הסופית, הרי הרצון לקבל שבו פועל בו, גם הרגש זולתו. ואם תרצה לידע בדיוק נמרץ, כמה הוא ההפרש מבחי"ג בחינה ג' של הרצון לקבל, שבמין החי, עד הבחי"ד בחינה ד' של הרצון לקבל שבמין האדם. אומר לך, שהוא כמו ערך בריה אחת של המציאות כלפי כל המציאות כולו [טבלה 2#].

#2 טבלה
דרגות של רצון לקבל

דצח"מ	רצון לקבל	בחינה
דומם	רצון קטן	בחינה א'
צומח	רצון גדול	בחינה ב'
חי	רצון יותר גדול	בחינה ג'
מדבר	רצון לקבל אינסופי	בחינה ד'

The Desire to Receive in the Animal species, which does not include any feeling for another, cannot create deficiencies and needs within himself, except to the degree that it is ingrained in that being alone. This is not so in the case of the Human who feels also for others, so that he lacks all that the other has and is filled with jealousy to acquire the entire being that the other has. And if he has one portion, he wants two hundred, and so his deficiencies and needs keep growing and multiplying until he wants to swallow all the entities in the whole world [See Chart B, page 182].

What was the world created for?

39) We have explained the following: The entire purpose that the Creator wishes for from the whole Creation that He has created is to cause enjoyment to His created beings in order for them to recognize His truth and His greatness, and that they will receive from Him all the goodness and the pleasure that He prepared for them, in the degree that is explained in the scriptural passage: "My dearest son, Ephraim! For is he not my darling child? etc." (Jeremiah 31:20) Now you find clearly that this purpose would not apply to the Inanimate or the large globes such as the Earth and moon and the sun, and no matter their splendor and size as they may be. Nor would it occur through Vegetative species, nor through living species, for they lack the ability to feel the other even when it comes to other members of their own species, that they are similar to them, so how can the Divine emotion and its benefits apply to them.

[It applies to] the Human species, only after being prepared to feel for the other, [meaning] with regard to members of their own similar species. After engaging with the Torah and the Precepts, through which they transform their Desire to Receive into a Desire to Share, thus achieving Similarity of Form with their Maker, they receive all the degrees that were prepared for them in the Supernal Worlds, that are named *Nefesh* (Lower Soul), *Ruach* (Spirit), *Neshamah*

כי הרצון לקבל שבמין החי, החסר מהרגש זולתו, לא יוכל להוליד
חסרונות וצרכים אליו רק בשיעור המוטבע באותה הבריה, בלבדה
משא"כ מה שאין כן האדם שיש לו גם הרגש זולתו, נמצא חסר גם בכל
מה שיש לזולתו, ומתמלא קנאה לרכוש לו כל הישות שנמצאת
בזולתו. ואם יש לו מנה רוצה מאתים, וכן נמצאים חסרונותיו וצרכיו
הולכים ומתרבים עד שהוא רוצה לבלוע כל הישות שבעולם כולו
[ראו טבלה ב', עמוד 183].

בשביל מה נברא העולם?

לט) ואחר שנתבאר, שכל התכלית הנרצה להבורא ית' מכל הבריאה
אשר ברא, היא להנות לנבראיו, בכדי שיכירו אמיתיותו וגדולתו,
ויקבלו ממנו כל הטוב והנועם שהכין בעדם, ובשיעור המבואר
בכתוב, הבן יקיר לי אפרים אם ילד שעשועים וכו' הנך מוצא בבירור,
שהתכלית הזו לא תחול, לא על הדוממים והכדורים הגדולים כמו
הארץ והירח והשמש, ולוא יהיו זהרם ומדתם כמה שיהיו, ולא על
מין הצומח, ולא על מין החי, שהרי חסרים מהרגש זולתם אפילו
מבני מינם הדומים להם, ואיך יחול עליהם ההרגש האלקי והטבתו.

אלא רק מין האדם בלבדו, אחר שכבר יש בהם ההכנה של הרגש
זולתו כלפי בני מינם הדומים להם, הנה אחר העבודה בתורה ומצות,
שמהפכים הרצון לקבל שלהם לרצון להשפיע, ובאים בהשואת
הצורה ליוצרם, שאז מקבלים כל המדרגות שהוכנו להם בעולמות
העליונים, הנקראות נרנח"י נפש רוח נשמה חיה יחידה, שבזה נעשו

(Soul), *Chayah* (Life-Sustaining), and *Yechidah* (Oneness). In this, they become prepared to receive the purpose that was there in the Thought of Creation, so it follows that the purpose of the Thought of Creation of all the worlds was only for the sake of mankind.

Can we break through beyond our limitations?

40) I know that this [idea] is not acceptable at all to some of the philosophers, and they cannot agree that the human being, who in their eyes is so inferior and insignificant, is the center of all the great and sublime Creation. But [these philosophers] are similar to the worm that was born inside a radish, and it sits there and thinks that the entire world of the Creator is as bitter and as dark and as small as the radish it was born in.

But once [the worm] breaks through the outer shell of the radish and peeps outside the radish, it is astonished and says, "I thought that the whole world is the size of the radish which I was born in, and now I see before me a great, enlightened, mighty, and exceedingly beautiful world." In the same manner, all those who are caught up in the shell of their Desire to Receive which they were born with and who have never tried to receive the special remedy that are the Torah and the practical Precepts that are able to penetrate this hard shell, transforming it into the Desire to Give Pleasure to the Creator. It must surely be that they [the philosophers] have to conclude [that they are] insignificant and empty as they really are. Nor can they possibly conceive of a possibility that this entire great reality was created only for them.

Indeed, if they had engaged with the Torah and the Precepts in order to give pleasure to their Maker with all the appropriate purity, and they come to penetrate the shell of their Desire to Receive which they were born with and received the Desire to Share, their eyes would have opened immediately to see and to understand themselves as well as all the stages of wisdom and intelligence and

מוכשרים לקבל את התכלית שבמחשבת הבריאה. הרי שתכלית כוונת הבריאה של כל העולמות לא היתה אלא בשביל האדם.

אם אפשר לפרוץ אל מעבר למוגבלות שלנו?

מ) ויודע אני, שאין דבר זה מקובל כלל על דעת חלק מן הפילוסופים, ואינם יכולים להסכים, אשר אדם השפל והאפסי בעיניהם, יהיה המרכז של כל הבריאה הגדולה והנשאה. אבל הם דומים, כאותה התולעת שנולדה תוך הצנון, והיא יושבת שם וחושבת, שכל עולמו של הקב"ה הוא כל כך מר, וכל כך חשוך, וכל כך קטן, כמדת הצנון שהיא נולדה בו.

אבל ברגע שבקעה את קליפת הצנון, וחוטפת מבט מבחוץ לצנון, היא תמהה, ואומרת, אני חשבתי שכל העולם הוא כמדת הצנון שנולדתי בו, ועתה אני רואה לפני עולם גדול נאור אדיר ויפה להפליא. כן אותם המשוקעים בקליפת הרצון לקבל שלהם שבה נולדו, ולא ניסו לקבל התבלין המיוחדים, שהם תורה ומצות מעשיות, המסוגלות לבקוע קליפה קשה הזו, ולהפכה לרצון להשפיע נ"ר נחת רוח ליוצרו, ודאי הוא, שהם מוכרחים להחליט על אפסותם וריקנותם כמו שהם באמת, ולא יוכלו להעלות על הדעת שכל המציאות הגדולה הזו לא נבראה אלא בשבילם.

אכן אם היו עוסקים בתורה ומצות להשפיע נחת רוח ליוצרם בכל הטהרה הנאותה, ויבואו לבקוע לבקוע קליפת הרצון לקבל שנולדו בה, ויקבלו הרצון להשפיע, הלא תיכף היו עיניהם נפתחות, לראות ולהשיג את עצמם ואת כל המדרגות של החכמה והתבונה והדעת

clear knowledge, which are lovely and pleasant to the extreme and which were prepared for them in the Spiritual Worlds. And then they would themselves say what our sages said: "What does a good guest say? He says, 'all the effort that the house owner has gone through, he did so only for me.' (Tractate *Berachot*, 58a)"

הבהירה, החמודות והנעימות עד לכלות נפש, שהוכנו להם בעולמות הרוחניים, ואז היו אומרים בעצמם מה שאמרו חז"ל, אורח טוב מה הוא אומר, כל מה שטרח בעל הבית לא טרח אלא בשבילי (מסכת ברכות, דף נח', עמוד א').

Part Two:
Advanced Kabbalah

(If this part feels too much for you, feel free to skip to Part Three)

וזלק שני:

קּבלה לּמתקּדּמים

(אם החלק הזה כבד מדי בשבילך כדאי לדלג לחלק שלישי)

Chapter Six: The Complex Universe – Sefirot, Souls, Lights and Vessels

What elements build the universe?

41) And in the end, it still remains to be explained why man must have all these Supernal Worlds that the Creator created for him. What is his need for them?

You should know that existence of all the Worlds is generally divided into five, and these Worlds are called: (1) *Adam Kadmon* (Primordial Man), (2) *Atzilut* (Emanation), (3) *Beriah* (Creation), (4) *Yetzirah* (Formation), and (5) *Asiyah* (Action). Although each of them has countless details and each is the aspect of one of five *Sefirot*: *Keter* (Crown), *Chochmah* (Wisdom), *Binah* (Understanding), *Tiferet* [*ZA*] (Splendor), and *Malchut* (Kingdom). Because the World of *Adam Kadmon* is *Keter*; the World of *Atzilut* is Chochmah; the World of *Beriah* is *Binah*; the World of *Yetzirah* is *Tiferet* [*ZA*]; and the World of *Asiyah* is *Malchut*. And the Lights that are clothed with these Five Worlds are called [respectively]: *Yechidah* (Oneness), *Chayah* (Life-Sustaining), *Neshamah* (Soul), *Ruach* (Spirit), and *Nefesh* (Lower Soul) [Chart #3].

CHART #3

Reality is divided into five parts

WORLD	SEFIRAH	LIGHT
Adam Kadmon (Primordial Man)	*Keter* (Crown)	*Yechidah* (Oneness)
Atzilut (Emanation)	*Chochmah* (Wisdom)	*Chayah* (Life-Sustaining)
Beriah (Creation)	*Binah* (Understanding)	*Neshamah* (Soul)
Yetzirah (Formation)	*Tiferet* [*ZA*] (Splendor)	*Ruach* (Spirit)
Asiyah (Action)	*Malchut* (Kingdom)	*Nefesh* (Lower Soul)

פרק שישי: העולם המורכב - ספירות, נשמות, אורות וכלים

איזה אלמנטים מרכיבים את המציאות?

מא) ועדיין נשאר לבאר, סוף סוף למה לו לאדם כל אלו עולמות העליונים שברא ית' בשבילו, ואיזה צורך יש לו לאדם בהם.

וצריך שתדע שמציאות כל העולמות נחלקת לה' עולמות בדרך כלל. ונקראים: א) אדם קדמון, ב) אצילות, ג) בריאה, ד) יצירה, ה) עשיה. אמנם בכל אחד מהם יש פרטים עד אין קץ. והם בחינת ה' הספירות כח"ב כתר חכמה בינה תו"מ תפארת [זעיר אנפין] ומלכות. כי עולם א"ק אדם קדמון הוא כתר, ועולם האצילות הוא חכמה, ועולם הבריאה הוא בינה, ועולם היצירה הוא תפארת [זעיר אנפין], ועולם העשיה הוא מלכות. והאורות המלובשים באלו ה' עלמות נקראים יחידה, חיה, נשמה, רוח, נפש. [טבלה מס' 3].

<u>טבלה #3</u>
המציאות מתחלקת לחמישה חלקים

אורות	ספירה	עולם
יחידה	כתר	אדם קדמון
חיה	חכמה	אצילות
נשמה	בינה	בריאה
רוח	תפארת [זעיר אנפין]	יצירה
נפש	מלכות	עשיה

The Light of *Yechidah* (Oneness) shines in the World of *Adam Kadmon* (Primordial Man); the Light of *Chayah* (Life-Sustaining) in the World of *Atzilut* (Emanation); the Light of *Neshamah* (Soul) in the World of *Beriah* (Creation); the Light of *Ruach* (Spirit) in the World of *Yetzirah* (Formation); and the Light of *Nefesh* (Lower Soul) in the World of *Asiyah* (Action). And all these Worlds, as well as everything that is contained in them, are inclusive in the Holy Name (the Tetragrammaton): *Yud* and *Hei* and *Vav* and *Hei* and the tip of the letter *Yud*.

Because the first World, which is *Adam Kadmon* (Primordial Man), is beyond our grasp, we are therefore given only a hint through the tip of the letter *Yud* of the Holy Name. Therefore, we never speak about it; we only speak about the Four Worlds: *Atzilut* (Emanation), *Beriah* (Creation), *Yetzirah* (Formation), and *Asiyah* (Action). The letter *Yud* is the World of *Atzilut*; the [first] letter *Hei* is the World of *Beriah*; the letter *Vav* is the World of *Yetzirah*; and the last [lit. lower] letter *Hei* is the World of *Asiyah* [Chart #4].

CHART #4

Five parts of reality and the Holy Name (the Tetragrammaton)

WORLD	SEFIRAH	LIGHT	LETTER
Adam Kadmon	*Keter*	*Yechidah*	tip of the *Yud*
Atzilut	*Chochmah*	*Chayah*	*Yud*
Beriah	*Binah*	*Neshamah*	*Hei*
Yetzirah	*Tiferet [ZA]*	*Ruach*	*Vav*
Asiyah	*Malchut*	*Nefesh*	*Hei*

Why do we need such complex and complicated structure?

42) And by this, we have explained the Five Worlds, which contain the entire spiritual reality that is extended from the *Ein Sof* (Endless) all the way to This World. And [these Five Worlds] inclusive of each other, and within each of the Worlds contains the entirety of the

שאור היחידה מאיר בעולם אדם קדמון. ואור החיה בעולם האצילות. ואור הנשמה בעולם הבריאה. ואור הרוח בעולם היצירה. ואור הנפש בעולם עשיה. וכל אלו העולמות וכל אשר בהם, נכללים בהשם הקדוש י"ה ו"ה, וקוצו של יוד.

כי עולם הא' שהוא א"ק אדם קדמון אין לנו תפיסה בו, וע"כ ועל כן מרומז רק בקוצו של יוד של השם, וע"כ ועל כן אין אנו מדברים ממנו, ואנו מזכירים תמיד רק ד' עולמות אבי"ע אצילות, בריאה, יצירה, עשיה. והי' היא עולם אצילות וה' עולם הבריאה, ו' עולם היצירה, ה' תתאה תחתונה היא עולם עשיה. [טבלה מס' 4].

טבלה #4

חמשת חלקי המציאות ואותיות הויה

אותיות	אורות	ספירה	עולם
קוצו של י'	יחידה	כתר	אדם קדמון
י'	חיה	חכמה	אצילות
ה'	נשמה	בינה	בריאה
ו'	רוח	תפארת [זעיר אנפין]	יצירה
ה'	נפש	מלכות	עשיה

למה צריך מבנה מורכב כל כך?

מב) והנה נתבארו ה' עולמות שהם כוללים כל המציאות הרוחנית הנמשכת מא"ס ב"ה מאין סוף ברוך הוא עד עוה"ז העולם הזה. אמנם הם

Five Worlds, as was mentioned above, as well as the five *Sefirot*: *Keter* (Crown), *Chochmah* (Wisdom), *Binah* (Understanding), *Tiferet* [ZA] (Splendor), and *Malchut* (Kingdom), in which the five Lights of *Nefesh* (Lower Soul), *Ruach* (Spirit), *Neshamah* (Soul), *Chayah* (Life-Sustaining), and *Yechidah* (Oneness) are clothed and which correspond to the Five Worlds, as mentioned above.

And in addition to the five *Sefirot*—*Keter* (Crown), *Chochmah* (Wisdom), *Binah* (Understanding), *Tiferet* [ZA] (Splendor), and *Malchut* (Kingdom)—that are in every World, there are also four spiritual aspects—Inanimate, Vegetative, Animal, and the Speaking—in each World. There [in each World] the Human Soul is the aspect of Speaking, the angels are the aspect of the Animal in the World, the aspect of the Vegetative [in each World] is called Clothings, and the aspect of the Inanimate is referred to as Chambers [Chart #5]. And [the aspects] are considered as enveloping each other.

CHART #5

Five parts of reality: Worlds, *Sefirah*, Lights, Letters, Desires, Vessels

WORLD	SEFIRAH	LIGHT	LETTER	DESIRE	VESSEL
Adam Kadmon	Keter	Yechidah	Tip of Yud	Root	
Atzilut	Chochmah	Chayah	Yud	Speaking	Soul
Beriah	Binah	Neshamah	Hei	Animal	Angels
Yetzirah	Tiferet [ZA]	Ruach	Vav	Vegetative	Clothings
Asiyah	Malchut	Nefesh	Hei	Inanimate	Chambers

כלולים זה מזה, ויש בכל עולם מהם כללות ה' העולמות, כנ"ל. ה' ספירות כח"ב כתר חכמה בינה תו"מ תפארת [זעיר אנפין] ומלכות, שבהן מלובשים ה' אורות נרנח"י נפש רוח נשמה חיה יחידה, שהן כנגד ה' העולמות, כנ"ל.

ומלבד ה' הספירות כח"ב כתר חכמה בינה תו"מ תפארת [זעיר אנפין] ומלכות שבכל עולם ועולם יש גם ד' בחינות דצח"מ דומם צומח חי מדבר רוחניים אשר נשמת האדם היא בחינת מדבר אשר שם, ובחינות החי הן המלאכים שבאותו עולם, ובחינות הצומח נקראות בשם לבושים, ובחינות הדומם נקראות בשם היכלות. ונבחנות כמלבישות זו את זו.

טבלה #5

חמשת חלקי המציאות: עולמות, ספירות, אורות, אותיות, רצון

כלי	רצון	אותיות	אורות	ספירה	עולם
	שורש	קוצו של י'	יחידה	כתר	אדם קדמון
נשמות	מדבר	י'	חיה	חכמה	אצילות
מלאכים	חי	ה'	נשמה	בינה	בריאה
לבושים	צומח	ו'	רוח	תפארת [זעיר אנפין]	יצירה
היכלות	דומם	ה'	נפש	מלכות	עשיה

Meaning that the aspect of the Speaking, which are the souls of humans, is the clothing of the five *Sefirot*—*Keter* (Crown), *Chochmah* (Wisdom), *Binah* (Understanding), *Tiferet* [*ZA*] (Splendor), and *Malchut* (Kingdom)—which are the Divine aspect in that specific World. (The matter of the Ten *Sefirot* being Divine will be made clear further on in the entrance to the *Zohar*.) And the aspects of the Animal, which are the angels, is the clothing of the souls; and the vegetables, which are the Clothing, envelop (lit. clothes) the angels; and the aspects of the Inanimate, which are the Chambers, surround them all.

And the matter of this Clothing is approximated, in the sense that they serve each other and develop one from the other, in the same way that we have explained regarding the physical Inanimate, Vegetative, Animal, and Speaking in This World (see above, sections 35 and 38). As we have said there, the three aspects of Inanimate, Vegetative, and Animal did not emerge for their own sake, but only in order that the fourth aspect, which is the human species, would be able to evolve and rise by them. And therefore, their only role is to serve the human and to bring him benefit. This is so also in the Spiritual Worlds, where these three aspects—Inanimate, Vegetative, and Animal—emerged only in order to serve and benefit the Speaking aspect in the World, which is the Human Soul. Therefore, it is considered that these aspects all are the clothing of the Human Soul, meaning, for his benefit.

What is the mysterious point in every person's heart?

43) The moment a human being is born, he immediately gets the aspect of a *Nefesh* (Lower Soul) of Holiness. This is not the essence of the *Nefesh*, but the aspect of the Back of the *Nefesh*, which means its last aspect and which, because of its small size, is called "a point." And it is clothed inside the heart of a person, that is, in the aspect of the Desire to Receive within him, which manifests mainly in the person's heart [Chart #9].

כי בחינת המדבר, שהיא נשמות בני אדם מלבישות על ה' ספירות כח"ב כתר חכמה בינה תו"מ תפארת [זעיר אנפין] ומלכות, שהן אלקיות שבאותו עולם (וענין י' הספירות שהן אלקיות יתבאר להלן בהמבוא לספר הזהר). ובחינות החי שהן המלאכים, מלבישות על הנשמות, והצומח שהם הלבושים, מלבישים על המלאכים, ובחינות הדומם שהן היכלות, מסבבות על כולם.

וענין ההתלבשות הזו משוערת, בענין שהם משמשים זה לזה ומתפתחים זה מזה, כעין שבארנו בדצח"מ דומם צומח חי מדבר הגשמיים שבעוה"ז העולם הזה (לעיל אות ל"ה ל"ח), וכמו שאמרנו שם שג' הבחינות דומם צומח חי לא יצאו בשביל עצמם, אלא רק שתוכל הבחי"ד הבחינה ד' להתפתח ולהתעלות על ידיהן, שהיא מין האדם. וע"כ ועל כן אין תפקידן אלא לשמש את האדם ולהועילו, כן הוא בכל העולמות הרוחניים, אשר הג' בחינות דומם צומח וחי אשר שם, לא יצאו שם, אלא כדי לשמש ולהועיל את בחינת המדבר אשר שם, שהיא נשמת האדם. ע"כ על כן נבחן, שכולם מלבישים על נשמת האדם. שפירושו, לתועלתו.

מהי הנקודה המסתורית שבלב כל אחד מאתנו?

מג) והנה האדם בעת שנולד, יש לו תכף בחינת נפש דקדושה, ולא נפש ממש, אלא בחינת אחורים של הנפש, שפירושו בחינה אחרונה שלה, המכונה, מפאת קטנותה, בשם נקודה. והיא מלובשת בלב האדם, כלומר בבחינת רצון לקבל שבו, המתגלה בעיקרו בלבו של אדם [טבלה מס' 9].

And you should know this rule: Everything that applies to the entirety of reality applies also to every World, and even to every small part that can be detailed which exists in that World. And thus, just as there are Five Worlds in the entirety of reality, which are, as we have said earlier, the five *Sefirot—Keter* (Crown), *Chochmah* (Wisdom), *Binah* (Understanding), *Tiferet* [*ZA*] (Splendor), and *Malchut* (Kingdom)—so also there are the five *Sefirot—Keter, Chochmah, Binah, Tiferet* [*ZA*], and *Malchut*—in each and every World. And there are five *Sefirot* in every small part of that World [Chart #6].

ודע הכלל הזה, שכל הנוהג בכלל המציאות כולו, נוהג בכל עולם,
ואפילו בכל חלק קטן שאך אפשר להפרט, שיש באותו עולם. באופן,
כמו שיש ה' עולמות בכלל המציאות, שהם ה' ספירות כח"ב כתר
חכמה בינה תו"מ תפארת [זעיר אנפין] ומלכות כנ"ל, כן יש ה' ספירות כח"ב
כתר חכמה בינה תו"מ תפארת [זעיר אנפין] ומלכות בכל עולם ועולם. וכן יש ה'
ספירות בכל חלק קטן שבאותו עולם [טבלה מס' 6].

CHART #6

Every World and every *Sefirah* is devided into the five parts of reality

WORLD/*SEFIRAH*	WORLD/*SEFIRAH*
Adam Kadmon / Keter	*Adam Kadmon / Keter*
	Atzilut / Chochmah
	Beriah / Binah
	Yetzirah / Tiferet [ZA]
	Asiyah / Malchut
Atzilut / Chochmah	*Adam Kadmon / Keter*
	Atzilut / Chochmah
	Beriah / Binah
	Yetzirah / Tiferet [ZA]
	Asiyah / Malchut
Beriah / Binah	*Adam Kadmon / Keter*
	Atzilut / Chochmah
	Beriah / Binah
	Yetzirah / Tiferet [ZA]
	Asiyah / Malchut
Yetzirah / Tiferet [ZA]	*Adam Kadmon / Keter*
	Atzilut / Chochmah
	Beriah / Binah
	Yetzirah / Tiferet [ZA]
	Asiyah / Malchut
Asiyah / Malchut	*Adam Kadmon / Keter*
	Atzilut / Chochmah
	Beriah / Binah
	Yetzirah / Tiferet [ZA]
	Asiyah / Malchut

<u>טבלה #6</u>

כל עולם וכל ספירה מכילים את חמשת חלקי המציאות

עולמות/ספירות	עולם/ספירה
אדם קדמון / כתר	
אצילות / חכמה	
בריאה / בינה	אדם קדמון / כתר
יצירה / תפארת [זעיר אנפין]	
עשיה / מלכות	
אדם קדמון / כתר	
אצילות / חכמה	
בריאה / בינה	אצילות / חכמה
יצירה / תפארת [זעיר אנפין]	
עשיה / מלכות	
אדם קדמון / כתר	
אצילות / חכמה	
בריאה / בינה	בריאה / בינה
יצירה / תפארת [זעיר אנפין]	
עשיה / מלכות	
אדם קדמון / כתר	
אצילות / חכמה	
בריאה / בינה	יצירה / תפארת
יצירה / תפארת [זעיר אנפין]	[זעיר אנפין]
עשיה / מלכות	
אדם קדמון / כתר	
אצילות / חכמה	
בריאה / בינה	עשיה / מלכות
יצירה / תפארת [זעיר אנפין]	
עשיה / מלכות	

We have said that This World is divided into [four aspects]:
Inanimate, Vegetative, Animal, and the Speaking, which correspond
to the four *Sefirot* of *Chochmah* (Wisdom), *Binah* (Understanding),
Tiferet [*ZA*] (Splendor), and *Malchut* (Kingdom). The Inanimate
[aspect] corresponds to *Malchut*, the Vegetative corresponds to
Tiferet [*ZA*], the Animal corresponds to *Binah*, and the Speaking
corresponds to *Chochmah*. The root of all of them corresponds to
Keter (Crown) [Chart #7].

CHART #7

Sefirot and the levels of Desires

SEFIRAH	DESIRE
Keter	Root
Chochmah	Speaking
Binah	Animal
Tiferet [*ZA*]	Vegetative
Malchut	Inanimate

And as was said, every single part of any species in the Inanimate,
Vegetative, Animal, or the Speaking aspects also contains within
itself the four aspects of Inanimate, Vegetative, Animal, and the
Speaking. And thus, even one part of the Speaking species, that is,
even one person has within himself the aspects of the Inanimate,
Vegetative, Animal, and the Speaking, which are the four parts of
his Desire to Receive [Chart #8], within him. Within which the
point of the *Nefesh* (Lower Soul) of Holiness is clothed.

והנה אמרנו, שעוה"ז שהעולם הזה נחלק על דצח"מ דומם צומח חי מדבר, והם כנגד ד' הספירות ח"ב חכמה בינה תו"מ תפארת [זעיר אנפין] ומלכות: כי דומם נגד מלכות, וצומח נגד תפארת, וחי נגד בינה, ומדבר נגד חכמה, והשורש של כולם הוא נגד כתר [טבלה מס' 7].

טבלה #7

ספירות ודרגות הרצון

ספירה	רצון
כתר	שורש
חכמה	מדבר
בינה	חי
תפארת [זעיר אנפין]	צומח
מלכות	דומם

אמנם, כאמור, שאפילו פרט אחד מכל מין ומין שבדצח"מ דומם צומח חי מדבר, יש בו וג"כ גם כן ד' בחינות דצח"מ דומם צומח חי מדבר. באופן שגם בפרט אחד שבמין המדבר, דהיינו אפילו באדם אחד יש בו וג"כ גם כן דצח"מ דומם צומח חי מדבר, שהם ד' חלקי הרצון לקבל שבו [טבלה מס' 8], שבהם מלובשת הנקודה מן הנפש דקדושה.

CHART #8

Each level of Desire is divided into and contains all the four levels

Inanimate	Vegetative	Animal	Speaking
Speaking	Speaking	Speaking	Speaking
Animal	Animal	Animal	Animal
Vegetative	Vegetative	Vegetative	Vegetative
Inanimate	Inanimate	Inanimate	Inanimate
			the point of the *Nefesh* in the heart

What really happens to our soul when we are teenagers?

44) Before [a person is] 13 years of age, no awareness of the Point in his Heart can be imaginable. That Point in his Heart starts to grow and show its essence (lit. activity) only after 13 years, when he starts to engage with the Torah and the Precepts even if he does so without any *Kavanah* (directed consciousness)—that is, without love and awe as is appropriate to the one who serves the King— even also [if it is done] Not For its own Sake. This is because the Precepts do not need *Kavanah* (directed consciousness), and even actions without *Kavanah* (directed consciousness) are capable of purifying [a person's] Desire to Receive, although this would be only [purifying] the first level in him, which is called the Inanimate [Chart #9].

טבלה #8

כל דרגת רצון מכילה את כל בחינות הרצון

מדבר	חי	צומח	דומם
מדבר	מדבר	מדבר	מדבר
חי	חי	חי	חי
צומח	צומח	צומח	צומח
דומם	דומם	דומם	דומם
נקודת הנפש שבלב			

מה קורה לנשמה בגיל העשרה?

מד) ומטרם י"ג שנה לא יצויר שום גילוי אל הנקודה שבלבו. אלא
לאחר י"ג שנה, כשמתחיל לעסוק בתורה ומצות, ואפילו בלי שום
כונה, דהיינו בלי אהבה ויראה, כראוי למשמש את המלך, גם אפילו
שלא לשמה, מתחילה הנקודה שבלבו להתגדל ולהראות פעולתה.
כי מצות אינן צריכות כונה, ואפילו המעשים בלי כונה מסוגלים
לטהר את הרצון לקבל שלו. אלא רק בשיעור דרגה הא' שבו,
המכונה דומם [טבלה מס' 9].

CHART #9

The beginning of the growth after *Bar/Bat Mitzvah*

the point of the <u>*Nefesh*</u> (Lower Soul), the point in the heart is born with the person but starts to grow after *Bar/Bat Mitzvah*	
Level of desire of the Speaking (Human)	
	Speaking
	Animal
	Vegetative
actions without *Kavanah* (directed consciousness) purify only inanimate	Inanimate

And to the degree to which he purifies the Inanimate part of the Desire to Receive, to that same degree he extends and builds the 613 limbs of the Point in the Heart, which is the Inanimate [aspect] of the *Nefesh* (Lower Soul) of Holiness. And when all the 613 Precepts are completed, from the [Precepts'] aspect of the action, this completes all the 613 limbs of the Point in the Heart, which is the Inanimate of the *Nefesh* of Holiness, whose 248 spiritual organs are built through performing the 248 "Do" Precepts, and whose 365 spiritual tendons are built through performing the 365 "Do Nots" Precepts. [This goes on] until it becomes a complete *Partzuf (Spiritual Structure, [lit. Face])* [Chart #10] of the *Nefesh* of Holiness, and then the *Nefesh* ascends and is the Clothing of the *Sefirah* of *Malchut* (Kingdom), which is in the spiritual World of *Asiyah* (Action) [Chart #11].

טבלה #9

התחלת הגדילה בגיל בר\בת מצווה

נקודת הַנֶפֶשׁ, הנקודה שבלב, נולדת עם האדם אבל מתחילה לגדול רק מגיל בר/בת מצווה	
דרגת הרצון לקבל של המדבר	
מדבר	
חי	
צומח	
דומם	מעשה ללא כוונה מטהר רק את חלק הדומם

ובשיעור שמטהר חלק הדומם של הרצון לקבל, בשיעור הזה הוא הולך ובונה את התרי"ג [365] אברים של הנקודה שבלב שהיא הדומם דנפש דקדושה. וכשנשלם בכל תרי"ג [613] מצות, מבחינת המעשה, נשלמו בזה כל תרי"ג [613] אברים של הנקודה שבלב, שהיא הדומם דנפש דקדושה, שרמ"ח [248] איבריה הרוחניים נבנים ע"י קיום רמ"ח [248] מצות עשה, ושס"ה [365] גידיה הרוחניים נבנים ע"י קיום שס"ה [365] מצות לא תעשה. עד שנעשית לפרצוף שלם [טבלה 10] דנפש דקדושה ואז הנפש עולה ומלבשת את ספירת המלכות, אשר בעולם עשיה הרוחני [טבלה מס' 11].

101

CHART # 10

The structure of a Spiritual vessel

Partzuf is a full Spiritual Structure built from 5 *Sefirot*/Worlds/levels of Desire			
	SEFIRAH	**WORLD**	**DESIRE**
	Keter	*Adam Kadmon*	Root
	Chochmah	*Atzilut*	Speaking
PARTZUF	*Binah*	*Beriah*	Animal
	Tiferet [ZA]	*Yetzirah*	Vegetative
	Malchut	*Asiyah*	Inanimate

CHART #11

The process of building the *Partzuf* of *Nefesh*

The Point of *Nefesh* of a person is born with him, but this Point in the Heart starts to act and grow only after *Bar/Bat Mitzvah*. It purifies the Inanimate and builds the 613 spiritual limbs to builds a full complete *Partzuf* of *Nefesh*.

Purifing the Inanimate level (By the point of the heart)	Building the 613 limbs through 248 "Do" preceps and 365 "Do not do" Precepts	A complete *Partzuf* of *Nefesh* includes: Inanimate, Vegetative, Animal and Speaking of *Malchut*	*Sefirah* *Malchut* (Kingdom) of the world of *Asiyah* (Action)	Inanimate, Vegetative and Animal of *Malchut* help build the *Partzuf* of *Nefesh*

טבלה #10

מבנה של כלי רוחני שלם (פרצוף)

	רצון	ספירה	עולם
פרצוף הוא מבנה של כלי רוחני שלם, הבנוי מחמש ספירות/עולמות/דרגות רצון			
	רצון	ספירה	עולם
פרצוף	שורש	כתר	אדם קדמון
	מדבר	חכמה	אצילות
	חי	בינה	בריאה
	צומח	תפארת [זעיר אנפין]	יצירה
	דומם	מלכות	עשיה

טבלה #11

בניית פרצוף הנפש

נקודה מאור הנפש של האדם נולדת עם האדם. אבל הנקודה הזו שבלב מתחילה לפעול רק מגיל בר\בת מצווה, והיא מטהרת את החלק הדומם של האדם ובונה איברים רוחניים עד בניית פרצוף שלם של אור הנפש

| דומם, צומח, חי של המלכות עוזרים לבנות פרצוף שלם של אור הנפש | ספירת מלכות בעולם עשיה | פרצוף שלם של אור הנפש כולל: דומם צומח חי ומדבר של הנפש | בניית תרי"ג האיברים על ידי רמ"ח מצוות "עשה" ושס"ה מצוות "לא תעשה" | טהור דרגת הדומם (על ידי הנקודה שבלב) |

And all the individual parts of the Spiritual, Inanimate, Vegetative, and Animal [aspects] of that World that are corresponding to that *Sefirah* of *Malchut* (Kingdom) of [the World of] *Asiyah* (Action), are in the service of, and assist the *Partzuf* (Spiritual Structure) of the *Nefesh* (Lower Soul) of the man who has ascended there, and that is to the degree that the *Nefesh* comprehend them. And this comprehension becomes like spiritual nourishment for it [the *Nefesh*], which gives it strength to increase and grow to the point that it can draw the Light of the *Sefirah* of *Malchut* of [the World of] *Asiyah* with all the perfection that is desired, and can shine inside the body of the Human. And this complete Light helps the person so he can add more effort to do his work with the Torah and the Precepts, and to receive all the remaining stages.

As we have said (verse 43), in the instant of the birth of the person's body, a point from the Light of the *Nefesh* (Lower Soul) is born and becomes clothed with him [person's body]. So too, here, when the *Partzuf* (Spiritual Structure) of the *Nefesh* of Holiness is completed [lit. born], a point from a higher stage from her is born with it, namely the last aspect of the Light of *Ruach* (Spirit) of *Asiyah* (Action), which becomes clothed with the interior of the *Partzuf* of the *Nefesh* [Chart #12]. And so it is with all the stages. With every stage that is born, the last aspect of the stage above it is immediately extended to it because this is the entire connection between the higher [stage] and lower one all the way up to the highest stage. And it is by virtue of that point that is within it—from its higher [level]—it becomes capable of ascending to a higher stage. There is nothing to expand any further.

וכל פרטי דומם צומח חי הרוחניים שבעולם ההוא, הנמצאים כנגד ספירת המלכות ההיא דעשיה, משמשים ומסייעים את פרצוף הנפש דאדם שעלה שם דהיינו בשיעור שהנפש משכלת אותם, שהמושכלות ההן נעשות לה מזון רוחני, הנותן לה כח להתרבות ולהתגדל עד שתוכל להמשיך אור ספירת המלכות דעשיה בכל השלמות הרצויה ולהאיר בגוף האדם. ואור

וכמו שאמרנו, שתכף עם לידת גופו של האדם נולדה ומתלבשת בו נקודה מאור הנפש [ראו סעיף מג'], כן כאן, כשנולד [ונשלם] לו פרצוף הנפש דקדושה, נולדת עמה גם נקודה ממדרגה העליונה ממנה, דהיינו בחינת אחרונה מאור הרוח דעשיה, המתלבשת בפנימיות פרצוף הנפש [טבלה מס' 12], וכך הוא הדרך בכל המדרגות שכל מדרגה שנולדה, יוצאת בה תכף בחינה אחרונה ממדרגה העליונה אליה. כי זה כל הקשר בין עליון לתחתון עד רום המעלות. וכך בסגולת נקודה זו שיש בה מעליונה, היא נעשית מסוגלת לעלות למדרגה העליונה ואכמ"ל ואין כאן מה להוסיף.

CHART #12

Completion of the *Partzuf* of *Nefesh* and birth of the *Partzuf* of *Ruach*.

Complete *Partzuf* of *Nefesh* that includes:	Speaking of *Nefesh*
	Animal of *Nefesh*
	Vegetative of *Nefesh*
	Inanimate of *Nefesh*
Point of the Light of *Ruach* (higher) is born with the completion of the *Partzuf* of *Nefesh* (lower). This point connects the Higher to the Lower World.	

What is the "Light of the *Nefesh* (Lower Soul)"?

45) And this Light of the *Nefesh* (Lower Soul) is referred to as the Light of the Inanimate [Chart #9] of Holiness of the World of *Asiyah* (Action), and it corresponds to the purified side of the Inanimate part of the Desire to Receive that exists in the body of the person, as mentioned above. Also, the action of its illumination in spirituality is similar to the aspect of the Inanimate species in the physical world, which we have explained above (section 35), since it [the Inanimate] does not have any individual movement of its parts but only an overall movement which includes all the parts equally. And it is the same with the Light of the *Partzuf* (Spiritual Structure) of the *Nefesh* of *Asiyah*. Even though it has 613 limbs, which are the 613 kinds of Differences of Form in the ways of receiving the abundance, still these differences cannot be discerned in it, but only a general Light whose action surrounds all of them equally, without recognizing its particulars.

What is the spiritual "dimmer" that quantifies our energy?

46) And you should know that even though the *Sefirot* are Divine and there is no dissimilarity or difference [in form] from the head

טבלה #12

שלימות פרצוף הנפש ולידת פרצוף הרוח.

	פרצוף שלם של אור <u>הנפש</u> כולל:
מדבר של הנפש	
חי של הנפש	
צומח של הנפש	
דומם של הנפש	
נקודה מאור <u>הרוח</u> (הגבוה יותר) נולדת מיד עם השלמת פרצוף הנפש (הנמוך יותר). נקודה זו מקשרת בין העליון והתחתון.	

מהו אור הנפש?

מה) ואור הנפש הזה מכונה בשם אור הדומם דקדושה דעולם עשיה. והוא להיותו מכוון נגד הטהרה של חלק הדומם [טבלה מס' 9] מהרצון לקבל שבגוף האדם כנ"ל. וכן פעולת הארתה ברוחניות דומה לבחי' בחינת מין הדומם שבגשמיות, שנתבאר לעיל (אות ל"ה) שאין לו תנועה פרטית לחלקיו אלא רק תנועה כוללת מקיפה לכל הפרטים בשוה, כן האור של פרצוף הנפש דעשיה, אע"פ ואף על פי שיש בו תרי"ג [613] אברים, שהם תרי"ג [613] מיני שינוי צורות בדרכי קבלת השפע, מ"מ מכל מקום אינם נכרים בו אלו השינוים, אלא רק אור כולל שפעולתו מקיפה את כולם בשוה, בלי הכר הפרטים שבו.

מהו ה"דימר" הרוחני שקוצב את עוצמת האור?

מו) ודע אע"פ ואף על פי שהספירות הן אלקיות ואין בהן שום שינוי והבדל מראש הכתר שבעולם א"ק אדם קדמון עד סוף ספירת המלכות

of the [*Sefirah*] of *Keter* (Crown) in the world of *Adam Kadmon* (Primordial Man) to the end of the *Sefirah* of *Malchut* (Kingdom) in the World of *Asiyah* (Action), still there is a great difference from the point of view of those who receive. [This is] because the *Sefirot* have two aspects—that of Lights and that of Vessels—and the Light in the *Sefirot* is complete Divinity, as mentioned above. However, the Vessels, which are called *Keter* (Crown), *Chochmah* (Wisdom), *Binah* (Understanding), *Tiferet* [*ZA*] (Splendor), and *Malchut* (Kingdom), are not considered Divinity in each of the three Lower Worlds referred to as *Beriah* (Creation), *Yetzirah* (Formation), and *Asiyah* (Action). Rather, they [the Vessels] are like covering [layers] that conceal the Light of *Ein Sof* (Endless) within themselves, and they determine the rate and degree of His Illumination towards the receivers, so that each of them will only receive in accordance with the degree of his purity.

From this aspect, even though the Light itself is One, still we refer to the Lights in the *Sefirot* by the terms: *Nefesh* (Lower Soul), *Ruach* (Spirit), *Neshamah* (Soul), *Chayah* (Life-Sustaining) and *Yechidah* (Oneness) [Chart #13], since the Light is divided according to the properties of the Vessels. Because *Malchut* (Kingdom) is the coarsest covering [layer] that conceals the Light of the Endless, and the Light that it [*Malchut*] transfers on from Him to those who receive it is only a small proportion [of the Endless Light] that is associated to the degree of purity in the Inanimate part of the human body alone, and therefore it [that Light] is called *Nefesh* (Lower Soul).

And the Vessel of *Tiferet* [*ZA*] (Splendor) is purer than the Vessel of *Malchut* (Kingdom), and the Light that it transfers from the Endless is associated to the degree of purity of the Vegetative part of the human body because it [the Vessel of *Tiferet* [*ZA*]] functions as more than just the Light of *Nefesh* (Lower Soul), and [this Light] is called the Light of *Ruach* (Spirit). And the Vessel of *Binah* (Understanding) is purer than [the Vessel of] *Tiferet* [*ZA*] (Splendor), and the Light that it transfers from the Endless is

שבעולם עשיה, מ"מ מכל מקום יש הבדל גדול כלפי המקבלים. כי
הספירות נבחנות לאורות וכלים, והאור שבספירות הוא אלקיות
גמורה, כנ"ל, אבל הכלים, הנקראים כח"ב כתר חכמה בינה ותו"מ תפארת
ומלכות, שבכל עולם מג' עולמות התחתונים הנקראים בריאה יצירה
עשיה. אינם בחינת אלקיות, אלא הם בחינת כיסוים המעלימים אור
א"ס ב"ה אין-סוף ברוך הוא שבתוכם, ומודדים קצבה ושיעור אל הארתו,
כלפי המקבלים, שכל אחד מהם יקבל רק לפי שיעור הטהרה שבו.

ומבחינה זו, אע"פ ואף על פי שהאור עצמו אחד הוא, מכל מקום אנו
מכנים האורות שבספירות בשם נרנח"י נפש רוח נשמה חיה יחידה [טבלה
מס' 13]. כי האור מתחלק לפי תכונות הכלים. כי המלכות, היא
הכיסוי היותר עב, המעלמת על אור א"ס ב"ה אין-סוף ברוך הוא, והאור
שהיא מעבירה ממנו ית' יתברך למקבלים הוא רק בשיעור קטן,
המיוחס לטהרת הדומם של גוף האדם לבד, וע"כ ועל כן נק' נקרא
נפש.

והכלי דת"ת תפארת הוא יותר זך מכלי המלכות, והאור שהוא מעביר
מא"ס ב"ה מאין-סוף ברוך הוא מיוחס לטהרת חלק הצומח דגוף האדם,
כי פועל בו יותר מאור הנפש, ונקרא אור הרוח, וכלי דבינה יותר זך
מת"ת תפארת, והאור שהוא מעביר מא"ס ב"ה מאין-סוף ברוך הוא, מיוחס
לטהרת חלק החי שבגוף האדם, ונקרא אור הנשמה. והכלי דחכמה
זך מכולם, והאור שהוא מעביר מא"ס ב"ה מאין-סוף ברוך הוא מיוחס

associated to the degree of purity of the Animal part in the human body, and [this Light] is called the Light of the *Neshamah* (Soul). And the Vessel of *Chochmah* (Wisdom) is purer than all of them, and the Light that it transfers from the Endless is associated with the degree of purity of the Speaking part in the body of man, and it is called the [Chart #13] Light of *Chayah* (Life-Sustaining), and its action is immeasurable, as we shall see.

CHART #13

Purity and coarseness of the five parts of reality

SEFIRAH	PURITY	LIGHT	DESIRE
Keter	Most pure	*Yechidah*	
Chochmah	Purer	*Chayah*	Speaking
Binah	Pure	*Neshamah*	Animal
Tiferet [ZA]	Less coarse	*Ruach*	Vegetative
Malchut	Coarse	*Nefesh*	Inanimate

What is the "Light of the Spirit"?

47) As was said above, in the *Partzuf* (Spiritual Structure) of *Nefesh* (Lower Soul) that the person has gained by virtue of engaging with the Torah and the Precepts without *kavanah* (meditation) the point of the Light of *Ruach* (Spirit) is already clothed there [see chart #12]. When a person strengthens himself to engage with the Torah and the Precepts with the proper *kavanah* (meditation), he keeps purifying the Vegetative part of the Desire to Receive in him [see chart #14], and to that extent, he goes on building the point of *Ruach* (Spirit) into the aspect of a *Partzuf* [in and of itself].

לטהרת חלק המדבר שבגוף האדם. ונקרא אור חיה [טבלה מס'
13]. שלפעולתו אין שיעור. כמו שיתבאר לפנינו.

<u>טבלה 13#</u>

מהו ועביות של חמשת חלקי המציאות

ספירה	אורות	זכות	רצון
כתר	יחידה	הכי זך	שורש
חכמה	חיה	יותר זך	מדבר
בינה	נשמה	זך	חי
תפארת [זעיר אנפין]	רוח	פחות עב	צומח
מלכות	נפש	הכסוי היותר עב	דומם

מהו אור הרוח?

מז) וכאמור שבפרצוף הנפש, שקנה האדם בכח העסק בתורה
ומצות שלא בכונה כבר מלובשת שם נקודה מאור הרוח [ראה
טבלה מס' 12], ובהתחזק האדם לעסוק בתורה ומצות בכונה
הרצויה, הולך ומטהר את החלק הצומח מבחי' רצון לקבל שבו
[טבלה מס' 14], ובשיעור הזה הוא הולך ובונה את הנקודה דרוח
לבחינת פרצוף [בפני עצמו].

CHART #14

The point of the *Ruach* (Spirit) purifies the Vegetative aspect.

The point of the <u>*Ruach*</u> (Spirit), which was born with the completion of the *Partzuf* of *Nefesh* (Lower Soul) purifies the <u>Vegetative</u> aspect of the Desire.	
Level of desire of the Speaking (Human)	
	Speaking
	Animal
Keeping Torah and Precepts with the proper *kavanah* (meditation)	Vegetative
	Inanimate

So, by [means of] the 248 "you shall do" Precepts performed with *kavanah* (meditation), the point expands throughout its 248 spiritual limbs. And through fulfilling the 365 "you shall not do" Precepts, the point expands in its 365 tendons. And when [the point] has completed [its full expansion] in all the 613 limbs, it ascends and enclothes the *Sefirah* of *Tiferet* [*ZA*] (Splendor) in the spiritual World of *Asiyah* (Action), which transmits to it, from the Endless, a more significant Light called "the Light of *Ruach* (Spirit)," which is associated to the [degree] of purity in the Vegetative part in the human body [Chart #15].

טבלה #14

נקודת הרוח מטהרת את חלק הצומח

נקודת <u>הרוח</u>, שנולדה עם השלמת פרצוף הנפש, מטהרת את חלק <u>הצומח</u> באדם	
דרגת הרצון לקבל של המדבר	
	מדבר
	חי
קיום תורה ומצוות בכוונה	צומח
	דומם

שע"י על ידי רמ"ח [248] מצות עשה בכוונה, מתפשטת הנקודה ברמ"ח [248] אבריה הרוחניים. וע"י על ידי קיום שס"ה [365] מצות לא תעשה, מתפשטת הנקודה בשס"ה [365] גידיה. וכשנשלמת בתרי"ג [613] האברים כולם, היא עולה ומלבשת את ספירת התפארת [זעיר אנפין] שבעולם העשיה הרוחני, המעבירה לו מא"ס ב"ה מאין-סוף ברוך הוא, אור יותר חשוב, הנק' נקרא אור הרוח, שהוא מכוון לפי טהרת חלק הצומח שבגוף האדם [טבלה #15].

113

CHART #15

Building the *Partzuf* of *Ruach*

The point of <u>Ruach</u> of a person was born with the completion of th *Partzuf* of *Nefesh*. The point purifies the <u>Vegetative</u> part and fulfills the 613 spiritual limbs that build a full complete *Partzuf* of Light of *Ruach*.				
Purifing the <u>Vegetative</u> level by the point of *Ruach*	Building the 613 limbs through 248 "Do" Preceps and 365 "Do not do" Precepts	A complete *Partzuf* of *Ruach* includes: Inanimate, Vegetative, Animal and Speaking of *Ruach*	*Sefirah Tiferet* [ZA] of the World of *Asiyah*	*Sefirah Tiferet* [ZA] helps build the *Partzuf* of *Ruach*

All the particulars of the Inanimate, Vegetative, and Animal [aspects] in the World of *Asiyah* (Action), which are associated to the stature of *Tiferet* [ZA] (Splendor), supports the *Partzuf* (Spiritual Structure) of *Ruach* (Spirit) of a person to receive the Lights from the *Sefirah* of *Tiferet* [ZA] with all its perfection, in the same way that was made clear above [with reference to] the Light of *Nefesh* (Lower Soul). Study that. For this reason, it [this *Partzuf* of *Ruach*] is called Vegetative of Holiness. And so the nature of its illumination is the same as the physical Vegetative [aspect], which has been explained above, inasmuch as it already has individual change in movement that can be discerned in each and every individual member of that domain, independently [see 36].

טבלה #15

בניית פרצוף הרוח

טהור	בניית תרי"ג	פרצוף שלם	ספירת	ספירת
דרגת	האיברים על	של אור	תפארת	תפארת
הצומח	ידי רמ"ח	הרוח כולל:	(ז"א)	עוזרת
על ידי	מצוות "עשה"	דומם צומח	בעולם	לבנות
הנקודה	ושס"ה מצוות	חי ומדבר	עשיה	פרצוף
של אור	"לא תעשה"	של הרוח		שלם
הרוח				של אור
				הרוח

נקודה מאור הרוח של האדם נולדה מיד עם השלמת פרצוף הנפש, הנקודה מטהרת את החלק הצומח של האדם ובונה איברים רוחניים עד בניית פרצוף שלם של אור הרוח

וכל פרטי דומם צומח וחי שבעולם עשיה המתיחסים לקומת התפארת [זעיר אנפין] מסייעים לפרצוף הרוח של האדם לקבל האורות מספירת התפארת [זעיר אנפין] בכל השלמות, על דרך שנתבאר לעיל באור הנפש, ע"ש עיין שם ומכונה משום זה, צומח דקדושה, וכן טבע הארתו כערך צומח הגשמי, שנתבאר לעיל, שכבר יש לו שינויי תנועה הניכרים בכל פרט ופרט שבו לפי עצמו.

And therefore, the Light of the spiritual Vegetative [aspect] whose power is already great enough to shine in special ways upon each and every one of the limbs of the 613 limbs that are in the *Partzuf* (Spiritual Structure) of *Ruach* (Spirit). Each and every one of them demonstrates a force that is attributed to that limb. And together with the emerging of the *Partzuf* of *Ruach*, a point of the next higher stage above it also emerged. This is the point of Light of *Neshamah* (Soul) [see chart #16], that is clothed within its [the *Partzuf* of *Ruach*] internal part.

CHART #16

Completion of the *Partzuf* of *Ruach* and birth of *Partzuf* of *Neshamah*

Complete *Partzuf* of *Ruach* that includes:	Speaking of *Ruach*
	Animal of *Ruach*
	Vegetative of *Ruach*
	Inanimate of *Ruach*
Point of the light of *Neshamah* (Higher) is born with the completion of the *Partzuf* of *Ruach* (Lower). This point connects the Higher to the Lower World	

What is the "Light of the Soul"?

48) And through engaging with the secrets of the Torah and with the taste (also: reason) of the Precepts, [the person] purifies the Animal part from the Desire to Receive that is in him [see chart #17]. And to the extent that he does this, he keeps on building the point of *Neshamah* (Soul) that is clothed inside him with its 248 [spiritual] limbs and 365 tendons. And when its construction is completed and it becomes a *Partzuf* (Spiritual Structure), then it ascends and becomes the clothing of the *Sefirah* of *Binah* (Understanding) in the spiritual World of *Asiyah* (Action) that this Vessel [*Binah*] is immeasurably purer then the first Vessels: *Tiferet* [ZA] (Splendor)

כן אור הצומח הרוחני כבר כחו גדול, להאיר בדרכים מיוחדים לכל אבר ואבר מתרי"ג [613] אברים שבפרצוף הרוח וכל אחד מהם מראה כח הפעולה המיוחס לאותו האבר. גם עם יציאת פרצוף הרוח יצאה עמו נקודה של המדרגה העליונה ממנו דהיינו נקודה של אור הנשמה [טבלה מס' 16], שהיא מתלבשת בפנימיותו.

טבלה #16

שלימות פרצוף הרוח ולידת פרצוף הנשמה.

מדבר של הרוח	**פרצוף שלם של אור הרוח כולל:**
חי של הרוח	
צומח של הרוח	
דומם של הרוח	
נקודה מאור <u>הנשמה</u> (הגבוה יותר) נולדת מיד עם השלמת פרצוף הרוח (הנמוך יותר). נקודה זו מקשרת בין העליון והתחתון.	

מהו אור הנשמה?

מח) וע"י ועל ידי העסק בסודות התורה ובטעמי מצות, הוא מטהר חלק החי מהרצון לקבל שבו [טבלה מס' 17], ובשיעור הזה הולך ובונה את נקודת הנשמה המלובשת בו ברמ"ח [248] אבריה ושס"ה [365] גידיה, וכשנשלמת בכל בנינה ונעשית פרצוף, אז עולה ומלבשת לספירת הבינה שבעולם העשיה הרוחני, שכלי זה הוא זך ביותר לאין ערך על כלים הראשונים תו"מ תפארת ומלכות, וע"כ ועל כן הוא מעביר לו אור גדול מא"ס ב"ה מאין-סוף ברוך הוא, הנקרא

and *Malchut* (Kingdom). And therefore it [the vessel of *Binah (Understanding)*] transfers [to the person] an immense Light from *Ein Sof* (Endless), called the Light of *Neshamah* (Soul). And all the particulars of the Inanimate, Vegetative and Animal aspects in the World of *Asiyah* (Action), which is associated with the stature of *Binah* (Understanding), are found serving and supporting the *Partzuf* of the *Neshamah* (Soul) of the person to receive his Lights perfectly from the *Sefirah* of *Binah* [see chart #18] in the way that has been explained with the Light of the *Nefesh* (Lower Soul); Study from there.

CHART #17

The point of the *Neshamah* (Soul) purifies the Animal aspect.

The point of the <u>Neshamah</u> (Soul), which was born with the with the completion of the *Partzuf* of *Ruach* (Spirit) purifies the <u>Animal</u> aspect of the Desire.	
Levels of Desire of the Speaking (Human)	
	Speaking
Keeping Torah and Precepts with the proper *kavanah* (meditation)	Animal
	Vegetative
	Inanimate

And the [*Partzuf* of the *Neshamah*] is also called the Animal aspect Animal of Holiness because it is intended for the purification of the Animal part in the human body. And this is the nature of its illumination, as was explained regarding the physical Animal species (see above, section 37) that gives an individual feeling to each and every one of the 613 limbs of the *Partzuf* (Spiritual Structure) because each one of [these limbs] is alive and feels with an independent sense of feeling without depending on the entire *Partzuf*. Thus it is considered that the 613 limbs in it [the *Partzuf*] are 613 *Partzufim* (Spiritual Structures) that are unique in the different types of their illumination, each one in its own [spatial] way.

אור הנשמה. וכל פרטי דומם צומח חי שבעולם עשיה, המיוחסים לקומת הבינה, נמצאים משמשים ומסייעים לפרצוף הנשמה של האדם, לקבל אורותיו בשלמות מספירת הבינה [טבלה מס' 18#], ע"ד על דרך שנתבאר באור הנפש ע"ש עיין שם.

טבלה 17#

נקודת הנשמה מטהרת את חלק החי

דרגת הרצון לקבל של המדבר	
נקודה מאור הנשמה, שנולדה עם השלמת פרצוף הרוח, מטהרת את חלק החי באדם	
מדבר	
חי	קיום תורה ומצוות בכוונה
צומח	
דומם	

והוא נק' ג"כ נקרא גם כן בחינת חי דקדושה, להיותו מכוון נגד טהרת חלק החי שבגוף האדם. וכן טבע הארתו, כדרך שנתבאר במין החי הגשמי (לעיל אות לז) שהוא נותן הרגשה פרטית לכל אבר ואבר מתרי"ג [613] אברי הפרצוף להיות חי ומרגיש בהרגשה חפשית לכל אחד מהם בלי שום התלות בכלל הפרצוף, עד שנבחן, שתרי"ג [613] אברים שבו הם תרי"ג [613] פרצופים המיוחדים במיני הארתם, כל אחד לפי דרכו.

CHART #18

Building the *Partzuf* of *Neshamah*

The point of <u>Neshamah</u> of a person was born with the completion of the *Partzuf* of *Ruach*. The point purifies the <u>Animal</u> part and fulfills the 613 spiritual limbs that build a full complete *Partzuf* of Light of *Neshamah*.

Purifing the <u>Animal</u> level by the point of *Neshamah*	Building the 613 limbs through 248 "Do" Preceps and 365 "Do not do" Precepts	A complete *Partzuf* of *Neshamah* includes: Inanimate, Vegetative, Animal and Speaking of *Neshamah*	*Sefirah Binah* of the World of *Asiyah*	*Sefirah Binah* helps build the *Partzuf* of <u>Neshamah</u>

And the quality of this Light over the Light of *Ruach* (Spirit) in spirituality is as the difference between the Animal species compared to the Inanimate and the Vegetative [aspects] in the physical reality. With the emergence of the *Partzuf* (Spiritual Structure) of *Neshamah* (Soul) a Point also emerges from the Light of *Chayah* (Life-Sustaining) of Holiness (which is the Light of the *Sefirah* of Chochmah). This [point] is clothed with [the *Partzuf*] its internal part [see chart #19].

<u>טבלה #18</u>

בניית פרצוף הנשמה

ספירת	ספירת	פרצוף	בניית	טהור
בינה	בינה בעולם	שלם	תרי"ג	דרגת
עוזרת	עשיה	של אור	האיברים	<u>החי</u>
לבנות		הנשמה	על ידי	על ידי
פרצוף		כולל:	רמ"ח	הנקודה
שלם		דומם	מצוות	של אור
של אור		צומח חי	"עשה"	הנשמה.
<u>הנשמה</u>		ומדבר	ושס"ה	
		של	מצוות	
		הנשמה	"לא	
			תעשה"	

נקודה מאור <u>הנשמה</u> של האדם נולדה מיד עם השלמת פרצוף הרוח, הנקודה מטהרת את החלק <u>החי</u> של האדם ובונה איברים רוחניים עד בניית פרצוף שלם של אור הנשמה

ומעלת אור הזה על אור הרוח ברוחניות, היא בערך הפרש מין החי כלפי הדומם וצומח בגשמיות. וכן יוצאת נקודה מאור החיה דקדושה (שהיא אור ספי' החכמה) עם יציאת פרצוף הנשמה ומתלבשת בפנימיותו [טבלה מס' #19].

CHART #19

Completion of the *Partzuf* of *Neshamah* (Soul) and birth of the *Partzuf* of *Chayah* (Life-Sustaining)

Complete *Partzuf* of *Neshamah* that includes:	Speaking of *Neshamah*
	Animal of *Neshamah*
	Vegetative of *Neshamah*
	Inanimate of *Neshamah*
Point of the Light of *Chayah* (Higher) is born with the completion of the *Partzuf* of *Neshamah* (Lower). This point connects the Higher to the Lower World	

How does the soul function and shine within the body?

49) And after [the person] has already merited that great Light that is called the Light of *Neshamah* (Soul) the 613 limbs in that *Partzuf* (Spiritual Structure) are already shining, every one of them in a complete and clear Light that is unique for it, like a special and unique *Partzuf* in itself. Then the possibility is opened for him to engage with each and every one of the Precepts in accordance with its true intended purpose because every limb in the *Partzuf* of the *Neshamah* shines to him the ways of every Precept that correlates to that limb. Then, empowered by the great force of those Lights, he goes on to purify the Speaking aspect of his Desire to Receive and transforms it into a Desire to Share [Chart #20].

טבלה 19#

שלימות פרצוף הנשמה ולידת פרצוף החיה.

	פרצוף שלם של אור <u>הנשמה</u> כולל:
מדבר של הנשמה	
חי של הנשמה	
צומח של הנשמה	
דומם של הנשמה	

נקודה מאור <u>החיה</u> (הגבוה יותר) נולדת מיד עם השלמת פרצוף הנשמה (הנמוך יותר). נקודה זו מקשרת בין העליון והתחתון.

איך מאירה הנשמה בתוך הגוף?

מט) ואחר שכבר זכה באור הגדול ההוא הנק' נקרא אור הנשמה, אשר תרי"ג [613] האברים שבפרצוף ההוא כבר מאירים כל אחד מהם באור שלם ובהיר המיוחד לו, כמו פרצוף מיוחד לעצמו, אז נפתח לו הפתח לעסוק בכל מצוה ומצוה על פי כונה אמיתית שבה, כי כל אבר של פרצוף הנשמה מאיר לו את דרכי כל מצוה המיוחסים לאותו אבר ובכחם הגדול של אורות ההם הוא הולך ומטהר את חלק המדבר שברצון לקבל שלו, ומהפכו לרצון להשפיע [טבלה 20#].

123

CHART #20

The point of the *Chayah* (Life-Sustaining) purifies the Speaking aspect.

The point of the _Chayah_ (Life-Sustaining), which was born with the completion of the *Partzuf* of *Neshamah* (Soul) purifies the <u>Speaking</u> aspect of the Desire.	
Levels of Desire of the Speaking (Human)	
Keeping Torah and Precepts with the proper *kavanah* (meditation)	Speaking
	Animal
	Vegetative
	Inanimate

And to that extent [of transformation], the point of the Light of *Chayah (Life-Sustaining)*, which is clothed in him, keeps on being constructed, with its 248 spiritual limbs and 365 spiritual tendons. And when it is completed into a whole *Partzuf* (Spiritual Structure), then it ascends and enclothes the *Sefirah* of *Chochmah* (Wisdom) of the spiritual World of *Asiyah* (Action). This Vessel is infinite in its purity, and therefore it passes on to him a great and enormous Light from the *Ein Sof* (Endless), which is called the Light of *Chayah* or the *Neshamah* of *Neshamah* (Soul of the Soul). And all the particular segments of the World of *Asiyah* (Action)—Inanimate, Vegetative, and Animal [aspects]—that relate to the *Sefirah* of *Chochmah* (Wisdom), help him to receive the Light of the *Sefirah* of Chochmah, in all its perfection, as was explained about the Light of the *Nefesh* (Lower Soul); study that (verse 45). And it is also called the point of the Speaking of Holiness because it corresponds to the purification of the Speaking aspect of the person.

טבלה #20

נקודת החיה מטהרת את חלק המדבר

נקודה מאור <u>החיה</u>, שנולדה עם השלמת פרצוף הנשמה, מטהרת את חלק <u>המדבר</u> באדם		
דרגת הרצון לקבל של המדבר		
מדבר	קיום תורה ומצוות בכוונה	
חי		
צומח		
דומם		

ובשיעור הזה הולכת ונבנית הנקודה של אור החיה המלובשת בו, ברמ"ח [248] איבריה ושס"ה [365] גידיה הרוחניים וכשנשלמת לפרצוף שלם, אז עולה ומלובשת לספירת החכמה שבעולם העשיה הרוחנית, אשר כלי זה אין קץ לזכות שבו, וע"כ וע"על כן הוא מעביר לו אור גדול ועצום מאד מא"ס ב"ה מאין-סוף ברוך הוא, הנק' נקרא אור החיה [טבלה#21] או נשמה לנשמה. וכל הפרטים שבעולם העשיה, שהם דומם וצומח וחי, המתיחסים לספירת החכמה, מסייעים לו לקבל אור ספירת החכמה בכל השלמות, ע"ד על דרך שנתבאר באור הנפש ע"ש עיין שם. וכן נק' נקרא מדבר דקדושה, להיותו מכוון נגד טהרת חלק המדבר שבגוף האדם.

CHART #21

Building the *Partzuf* of *Chayah* (Life-Sustaining)

The point of <u>Chayah</u> of a person was born with the completion of the *Partzuf* of *Neshamah*. The point purifies the <u>Speaking</u> part and fulfills the 613 spiritual limbs that build a full complete *Partzuf* of the Light of *Chayah* (*Neshamah of Neshamah*).				
Purifing the <u>Speaking</u> level by the point of <u>Chayah</u>	Building the 613 limbs through 248 "Do" Preceps and 365 "Do not do" Precepts	A complete *Partzuf of Chayah* includes: Inanimate, Vegetative, Animal and Speaking of *Chayah*	*Sefirah Chochmah* of the World of *Asiyah*	*Sefirah Chochmah* helps build the *Partzuf* of *Chayah*

And so is the significance of that Light in the Divine as the significance of the Speaking [aspect] in the physical Inanimate, Vegetative, Animal, and the Speaking [domains], that is to say, he gains the ability to feel the other. Meaning, that the extent of the dimension of that Light, [relative] to the dimension of the spiritual Inanimate, Vegetative, and Animal [domains] is as the extent of the dimension of the physical Speaking species in relation to the physical Inanimate, Vegetative, and Animal [domains]. And the aspect of the Light of the *Ein Sof* (Endless), which is clothed within this *Partzuf* (Spiritual Structure), is called the [point of the] Light of *Yechidah* (Oneness) [see chart #22].

טבלה #21

בניית פרצוף החיה (הנשמה של הנשמה)

נקודה מאור החיה של האדם נולדה מיד עם השלמת פרצוף הנשמה, הנקודה מטהרת את החלק המדבר של האדם ובונה איברים רוחניים עד בניית פרצוף שלם של אור החיה (נשמה לנשמה)				
ספירת חכמה עוזרת לבנות פרצוף שלם של אור החיה	ספירת חכמה בעולם עשיה	פרצוף שלם של אור החיה כולל: דומם צומח חי ומדבר של החיה	בניית תרי"ג האיברים על ידי רמ"ח מצוות "עשה" ושס"ה מצוות "לא תעשה"	טהור דרגת המדבר על ידי הנקודה של אור החיה.

וכן ערכו של האור ההוא באלקיות כערך המדבר שבדצח"מ דומם צומח חי מדבר הגשמיים, דהיינו שקונה הרגש זולתו. באופן ששיעור גדלו של אור ההוא על גודל דצ"ח דומם צומח חי הרוחניים כשיעור גדלו של מין המדבר הגשמי על דצ"ח דומם צומח חי הגשמיים. ובחינת אור א"ס ב"ה אין-סוף ברוך הוא המלובש בפרצוף זה, הוא נק' נקרא אור יחידה [טבלה מס' #22].

CHART #22

Completion of *Partzuf* of *Chayah* (Life-sustaining) and birth of *Partzuf* of *Yechidah* (Oneness)

Comlete *Partzuf* of *Chayah* that includes:	Speaking of *Chayah*
	Animal of *Chayah*
	Vegetative of *Chayah*
	Inanimate of *Chayah*
Point of the light of the Higher *Yechidah* (Oneness) is born with the completion of the lower *Partzuf* of *Chayah*. This point connects the Higher to the Lower world.	

טבלה #22

שלימות פרצוף החיה ולידת פרצוף היחידה.

	פרצוף שלם של אור <u>החיה</u> (נשמה של נשמה) כולל :
מדבר של החיה	
חי של החיה	
צומח של החיה	
דומם של החיה	

נקודה מאור <u>היחידה</u> (הגבוה יותר) נולדת מיד עם השלמת פרצוף החיה (הנמוך יותר). נקודה זו מקשרת בין העליון והתחתון.

Chapter Seven: Total Transformation

How do the five parts of the soul affect us?

50) You should know that these five aspects of Light—*Nefesh* (Lower Soul), *Ruach* (Spirit), *Neshamah* (Soul), *Chayah* (Life-Sustaining), and *Yechidah* (Oneness), which were received from the World of *Asiyah* (Action)—are only the *Nefesh, Ruach, Neshamah, Chayah*, and *Yechidah* of the Light of the *Nefesh*. They do not have anything in them pertaining to the Light of *Ruach* (Spirit) because the Light of *Ruach* is only in the World of *Yetzirah* (Formation), the Light of *Neshamah* is only in the World of *Beriah* (Creation), the Light of *Chayah* is only in the World of *Atzilut* (Emanation), and the Light of *Yechidah* is only in the World of *Adam Kadmon* (Primordial Man). But, like we said before [see chart #6], everything that is in the entire collective is also revealed in each and every individual to the smallest detail that could be detailed.

Therefore, all five aspects of *Nefesh* (Lower Soul), *Ruach* (Spirit), *Neshamah* (Soul), *Chayah* (Life-Sustaining), and *Yechidah* (Oneness) exist also in the World of *Asiyah* (Action), in the way that we have already explained, but they are only the *Nefesh, Ruach, Neshamah, Chayah*, and *Yechidah* [aspects] of the *Nefesh*. And exactly in the same way, all these five aspects — *Nefesh, Ruach, Neshamah, Chayah*, and *Yechidah* —are present in the World of *Yetzirah* (Formation), and they are only the five parts of the *Ruach*. And also all the five aspects, *Nefesh, Ruach, Neshamah, Chayah*, and *Yechidah* exist in the World of *Beriah* (Creation); they are the five parts of the *Neshamah* [see chart #23].

And so it is, in the World of *Atzilut* (Emanation) that are the five parts of the Light of *Chayah* (Life-Sustaining). So it is [too] in the World of *Adam Kadmon* (Primordial Man) that are the five parts of the Light of *Yechidah*. And the distinction between one World and another is the same as we explained when discussing the differentiations between each one of the *Nefesh* (Lower Soul), *Ruach* (Spirit), *Neshamah* (Soul), *Chayah* (Life-Sustaining), and *Yechidah* (Oneness) of the World of *Asiyah* (Action) [see chart #23].

פרק שביעי: ענני מווזלט

איך חמשת חלקי הנשמה משפיעים עלינו?

נ) אמנם תדע שכל אלו ה' בחינות האורות נרנח"י נפש רוח נשמה חיה יחידה שנתקבלו מעולם העשיה, אינן אלא בחינת נרנח"י נפש רוח נשמה חיה יחידה של אור הנפש, ואין בהן עוד מבחינת אור הרוח ולא כלום, כי אין אור הרוח אלא בעולם היצירה, ואור הנשמה רק בעולם הבריאה, ואור החיה רק בעולם אצילות, ואור היחידה רק בעולם א"ק אדם קדמון. אלא כמו שאמרנו לעיל [טבלה מס' 6#], שכל שיש בכלל כולו מתגלה ג"כ גם כן בכל הפרטים, עד הפרט היותר קטן שאך אפשר להפרט.

ולפיכך ישנן כל ה' בחינות נרנח"י נפש רוח נשמה חיה יחידה גם בעולם העשיה, כדרך שבארנו אותן, אבל הן רק נרנח"י נפש רוח נשמה חיה יחידה דנפש. וממש על דרך זה ישנן כל ה' בחינות נרנח"י נפש רוח נשמה חיה יחידה בעולם היצירה והן רק ה' חלקי הרוח. וכן ישנן כל ה' בחינות נרנח"י נפש רוח נשמה חיה יחידה בעולם הבריאה, והן ה' חלקי הנשמה [טבלה מס' 23#].

וכן הוא בעולם האצילות שהן ה' חלקי אור החיה. וכן הוא בעולם א"ק אדם קדמון שהן ה' חלקי אור היחידה. וההפרש שבין עולם לעולם, הוא ע"ד על דרך שבארנו בהבחנות שבין כל אחד מנרנח"י נפש רוח נשמה חיה יחידה דעשיה [טבלה מס' 23#].

CHART #23

Every World and every Light includes the five parts of the Soul

Worlds	Lights	Lights in details
Adam Kadmon	Yechidah (Oneness)	Yechidah of Yechidah
		Chayah of Yechidah
		Neshamah of Yechidah
		Ruach of Yechidah
		Nefesh of Yechidah
Atzilut	Chayah (Life-Sustaining)	Yechidah of Chayah
		Chayah of Chayah
		Neshamah of Chayah
		Ruach of Chayah
		Nefesh of Chayah
Beriah	Neshamah (Soul)	Yechidah of Neshamah
		Chayah of Neshamah
		Neshamah of Neshamah
		Ruach of Neshamah
		Nefesh of Neshamah
Yetzirah	Ruach (Spirit)	Yechidah of Ruach
		Chayah of Ruach
		Neshamah of Ruach
		Ruach of Ruach
		Nefesh of Ruach
Asiyah	Nefesh (Lower Soul)	Yechidah of Nefesh
		Chayah of Nefesh
		Neshamah of Nefesh
		Ruach of Nefesh
		Nefesh of Nefesh

טבלה #23

כל עולם וכל אור מכילים את חמשת חלקי הנשמה

עולמות ואורות	אור הנשמה	עולמות
יחידה של יחידה		
חיה של יחידה		
נשמה של יחידה	יחידה	אדם קדמון
רוח של יחידה		
נפש של יחידה		
יחידה של חיה		
חיה של חיה		
נשמה של חיה	חיה	אצילות
רוח של חיה		
נפש של חיה		
יחידה של נשמה		
חיה של נשמה		
נשמה של נשמה	נשמה	בריאה
רוח של נשמה		
נפש של נשמה		
יחידה של רוח		
חיה של רוח		
נשמה של רוח	רוח	יצירה
רוח של רוח		
נפש של רוח		
יחידה של נפש		
חיה של נפש		
נשמה של נפש	נפש	עשיה
רוח של נפש		
נפש של נפש		

What is the importance of total and everlasting transformation?

51) And you should know that the *teshuvah* (repentance) and purification is not acceptable unless it is completely permanent in a way that [the person] would never return back to his foolishness. According to the verse: "How do we know that *teshuvah* (repentance) [has been done]?"—"When He Who knows all Mysteries bears witness that [the sinner] will not return to his foolishness again." (According to *Psalms* 85:9) So, it came out that what we have said: That if a person purifies the Inanimate part of the Desire to Receive inherent in him, he gains the *Partzuf* (Spiritual Structure) of *Nefesh* (Lower Soul) of the World of *Asiyah* (Action) and he [then] ascends and covers (lit. clothes) the *Sefirah* of *Malchut* (Kingdom) of *Asiyah* [see chart #9]. This means that it is certain that this person will merit the purification of the Inanimate part in a complete, permanent way, so that he will not return to his foolishness anymore. And then he can ascend to the spiritual World of *Asiyah* (Action) because he has purity and absolute Similarity of Form with that World.

As for the rest of the stages that we mentioned that are *Ruach* (Spirit), *Neshamah* (Soul), *Chayah* (Life-Sustaining), and *Yechidah* (Oneness) of [the World of] *Asiyah* (Action)—one has to purify the Vegetative, Animal, and the Speaking aspects of his Desire to Receive, so that they can encloth and receive those Lights. This purification does not have to be completely permanent, that is, to the point that "He Who Knows all Mysteries bears witness that [the sinner] will not return to his foolishness again." The reason for this is that the entirety of the World of *Asiyah* (Action), with all the five *Sefirot* in it—*Keter* (Crown), *Chochmah* (Wisdom), *Binah* (Understanding), *Tiferet* [ZA] (Splendor) and *Malchut* (Kingdom)—is only an aspect of *Malchut*, which is associated with the purification of the Inanimate aspect alone. And the five *Sefirot* are only five parts of *Malchut*.

מה החשיבות של שני מוחלט וקבוע?

נא) ודע שהתשובה והטהרה אינה מקובלת זולת שתהיה בקביעות מוחלטת, שלא ישוב לכסלו עוד. וז"ש וזה שכתוב היכי דמי תשובה עד שיעיד עליו יודע תעלומות שלא ישוב לכסלו עוד. ונמצא, שמה שאמרנו, שאם אדם מטהר את חלק הדומם מהרצון לקבל שבו, שהוא זוכה לפרצוף נפש דעשיה ועולה ומלביש את ספירת המלכות דעשיה [טבלה מס' 9]. היינו ודאי שיזכה בטהרת חלק הדומם בקביעות מוחלטת באופן שלא ישוב לכסלו עוד. ואז יכול לעלות לעולם העשיה הרוחני, כי יש לו טהרה והשואת הצורה בהחלט, לעולם ההוא.

אמנם שאר המדרגות שאמרנו, שהן רוח נשמה חיה יחידה דעשיה, שצריך לטהר כנגדן את חלק הצומח והחי והמדבר מהרצון לקבל שלו, שילבישו ויקבלו האורות ההם. אין הטהרה צריכה להיות בקביעות מוחלטת, עד שיעיד עליו יודע תעלומות שלא ישוב לכסלו עוד. והוא מטעם, שכל עולם העשיה בכל ה' ספירות כח"ב תו"מ כתר חכמה ובינה בתפארת ומלכות שבו, אינם אלא בחינת מלכות לבד, שיחסה רק לטהרת הדומם בלבד. וה' הספירות, הן רק ה' חלקי המלכות.

How do we connect with the divine even with partial and temporary change?

Therefore, because [the person] had already merited the purification of the Inanimate part in his Desire to Receive, he already gained Similarity of Form with the entire World of *Asiyah* (Action). However, each and every *Sefirah* from the World of *Asiyah* (Action) receives from the aspect that corresponds to it in the Worlds higher than itself. For example, the *Sefirah* of *Tiferet* [*ZA*] (Splendor) of [the World of] *Asiyah* (Action) receives from the World of *Yetzirah* (Formation), which is entirely the aspect of *Tiferet* [*ZA*]; and the Light of *Ruach* (Spirit). [Similarly,] the *Sefirah* of *Binah* (Understanding) of [the World of] *Asiyah* (Action) receives from the World of *Beriah* (Creation), which is entirely the aspect of *Neshamah* (Soul). And the *Sefirah* of *Chochmah* (Wisdom) of [the World of] *Asiyah* (Action) receives from the World of *Atzilut* (Emanation), which is entirely *Chochmah*, and [is also] the Light of *Chayah* (Life-Sustaining).

Therefore, even if [a person] had purified only the Inanimate part permanently, nevertheless, if he has purified the other three parts of his Desire to Receive although not permanently, he can also receive *Ruach* (Spirit), *Neshamah* (Soul), and *Chayah* (Life-Sustaining) from *Tiferet* [*ZA*] (Splendor), *Binah* (Understanding) and *Chochmah* (Wisdom) of [the World of] *Asiyah* (Action) but just not permanently. Because as soon as one of the three parts of his Desire to Receive [namely, Vegetative, Animal, and the Speaking] is aroused again, he will lose those Lights immediately.

52) After he permanently purifies also the Vegetative part of his Desire to Receive, he then permanently ascends to the World of *Yetzirah* (Formation), where he permanently gains Light up to the level of *Ruach* (Spirit). He can also obtain there the Lights of *Neshamah* (Soul) and *Chayah* (Life-Sustaining) from the *Sefirot* of *Binah* (Understanding) and *Chochmah* (Wisdom) that resides there, which are considered the *Neshamah* of *Ruach* and the *Chayah* of

איך להתחבר לאור גם עם שנוי חלקי וזמני?

וע"כ ועל כן כיון שכבר זכה על כל פנים בטהרת חלק הדומם שברצון לקבל, כבר יש לו השואת הצורה לכל עולם העשיה, אלא, כיון שכל ספירה וספירה מעולם העשיה, מקבלת מהבחינה שכנגדה בעולמות העליונים ממנה. למשל ספירת הת"ת [זעיר אנפין] תפארת דעשיה מקבלת מעולם היצירה שכולו בחי' ת"ת [זעיר אנפין] תפארת, ואור הרוח. וספירת בינה דעשיה מקבלת מעולם הבריאה שכולו בחינת נשמה. וספירת חכמה דעשיה מקבלת מעולם האצילות שכולו חכמה, ואור החיה.

ולפיכך אע"פ ואף על פי שלא טיהר אלא חלק הדומם בקביעות, מ"מ מכל מקום אם טיהר שאר ג' חלקי הרצון לקבל שלו, עכ"פ על כל פנים שלא בקביעות, הוא יכול לקבל גם רוח נשמה חיה מת"ת מתפארת [זעיר אנפין] ובינה וחכמה דעשיה, אלא רק שלא בקביעות, כי בשעה שנתעורר שוב אחד מג' חלקי הרצון לקבל שלו, נמצא תכף מאבד את האורות ההם.

נב) ואחר שמטהר גם חלק הצומח שברצון לקבל שלו בבחי' קביעות הוא עולה לעולם היצירה בקביעות, ומשיג שם עד מדרגת הרוח בקביעות, ויכול להשיג שם גם האורות נשמה וחיה מספירות בינה וחכמה אשר שם, הנבחנות לנשמה דרוח וחיה דרוח, אפילו

Ruach, even before he merited to purify the part of the Animal and Speaking in an absolute and permanent way, as it was explained in the [case of] World of *Asiyah* (Action) but just not permanently.

Because after [the person] achieved permanent purification of the Vegetative [aspect of] the Desire to Receive within him, he is already in Similarity of Form with the entire World of *Yetzirah* (Formation) to the height of heights as was mentioned above in the World of *Asiyah*.

How do we attain Similarity of Form with the Celestial Worlds?

53) And after he also purifies the Animal part of his Desire to Receive and turns it into the Desire to Share, to the point where "He Who Knows all Mysteries bears witness that [the sinner] will not return to his foolishness again," he is already in Similarity of Form with the World of *Beriah* (Creation), and he ascends and permanently receives up to the level Light of *Neshamah* (Soul). Similarly, by purifying the Speaking part of [the Desire to Receive] in his body, he can ascend to the *Sefirah* of *Chochmah* (Wisdom) and receive also the Light of *Chayah* (Life-Sustaining) that resides there, even though he has not yet purified [the Speaking aspect] permanently. Likewise [it applies to the World of] *Yetzirah* (Formation) and in *Asiyah* (Action). But also the Light shines not permanently for him, as was mentioned above.

How do we achieve the greatest Light?

54) And when [the person] merits permanently purifying the Speaking part of his Desire to Receive, he then gains Similarity of Form with the World of *Atzilut* (Emanation) and ascends and receives there the Light of *Chayah* (Life-Sustaining) permanently. And when he gains more, he merits the Light of the *Ein Sof* (Endless) and the Light of *Yechidah* (Oneness) that clothes itself in the Light of *Chayah* (Life-Sustaining). And there is no need to add at this point.

מטרם שזכה לטהרת חלק החי והמדבר בבחינת קביעות מוחלטת,
ע"ד על דרך שנתבאר בעולם העשיה. אבל רק שלא בקביעות.

כי אחר שהשיג טהרת הצומח מרצון לקבל שבו, בבחינת הקביעות,
כבר הוא בהשואת הצורה לעולם היצירה כולו עד רום המעלות,
כנ"ל בעולם העשיה.

איך משיגים שווי צורה עם העולמות העליונים?

נג) ואחר שמטהר גם חלק החי מהרצון לקבל והופכו לרצון
להשפיע, עד שיודע תעלומות יעיד עליו שלא ישוב לכסלו עוד, כבר
הוא בהשואת הצורה לעולם הבריאה, ועולה ומקבל שם עד אור
הנשמה בקביעות. וגם ע"י על ידי טהרת חלק המדבר שבגופו יכול
לעלות עד ספירת החכמה ומקבל גם אור החיה אשר שם, אע"פ אף
על פי שעוד לא טיהר אותו בקביעות, כנ"ל ביצירה ועשיה. אבל גם
האור מאיר לו שלא בקביעות כנ"ל.

איך זוכים לאור הגדול ביותר?

נד) וכשזוכה לטהר בקביעות גם חלק המדבר מהרצון לקבל שבו,
אז זוכה להשואת הצורה לעולם האצילות, ועולה ומקבל שם אור
החיה בקביעות. וכשזוכה יותר, זוכה לאור א"ס אין סוף ואור היחידה
המתלבש באור החיה ואכמ"ל ואין כאן מה להוסיף.

How do we get assistance from the Upper Worlds?

55) And hereby it was explained well what we discussed above (in verse 41), when we asked why should a person know all these Upper Worlds that the Creator has created for him. And what need does a human being have for them? Now you can see that it is not possible for a person to give pleasure to his Maker without being aided by all these [Upper] Worlds.

And to the extent that he purifies his Desire to Receive, he will attain the Lights and stages of his soul that are called [from bottom to top]: *Nefesh* (Lower Soul), *Ruach* (Spirit), *Neshamah* (Soul), *Chayah* (Life-Sustaining), and *Yechidah* (Oneness). And [with] every stage that he attains, the Lights of that stage help him in his purification, and so he ascends in his stages until he merits reaching the pleasures of the Essence of the purpose of the Thought of Creation, as was mentioned above (in verse 33).

And this is what said in the *Zohar* (Noah verse 63) about the passage: "He who comes to purify himself receives assistance [from above]. And he asks: In what way is he being assisted? And the answer is that he is being assisted with the holy soul," study there. This is because it is not possible to reach the purification desired by the Thought of Creation, [it is possible] only through assistance from all the levels of our soul: *Nefesh* (Lower soul), *Ruach* (Spirit), *Neshamah* (Soul), *Chayah* (Life-sustaining), and *Yechidah* (Oneness), as explained above.

Why do we need to know the structure of the spiritual reality?

56) We should know that all these [levels of the Soul]—*Nefesh* (Lower Soul), *Ruach* (Spirit), *Neshamah* (Soul), *Chayah* (Life-Sustaining), and *Yechidah* (Oneness)—that we have spoken about so far are the five parts that all reality is divided into. Indeed, everything that applies to the entire collective applies even to the smallest detail of reality, as was mentioned above [in verse 42]. For

איך לקבל סיוע מהעולמות הרוחניים?

נה) והנה נתבאר היטב מה שעמדנו לעיל (באות מא), ששאלנו למה
לו לאדם כל אלו העולמות העליונים שברא השי"ת בשבילו, ואיזה
צורך יש לו לאדם בהם. כי עתה תראה, שאי אפשר כלל לאדם להגיע
לעשית נ"ר נחת רוח ליוצרו זולת על ידי סיועם של כל העולמות האלו.

כי בשיעור הטהרה של הרצון לקבל שבו משיג האורות והמדרגות
של נשמתו הנקראים נרנח"י נפש רוח נשמה חיה יחידה, וכל מדרגה
שמשיג, הרי האורות של אותו מדרגה מסייעים לו בטהרתו, וכן
עולה במדרגותיו עד שזוכה להגיע אל השעשועים של תכלית הכונה
שבמחשבת הבריאה. כנ"ל (אות לג).

וזה שאמרו בזהר (נח אות ס"ג) על המאמר הבא לטהר מסייעין
אותו, ושואל במה מסייעין אותו, ואומר שמסייעין אותו בנשמתא
קדישא נשמה קדושה. ע"ש עיין שם. כי אי אפשר לבא לטהרה הרצויה
למחשבת הבריאה, זולת ע"י על ידי סיוע כל המדרגות נרנח"י נפש
רוח נשמה חיה יחידה של הנשמה כמבואר.

מדוע צריך לדעת את מבנה העולמות?

נו) ויש לדעת שכל אלו נרנח"י נפש רוח נשמה חיה יחידה שדברנו עד הנה,
הרי הם ה' חלקים, שכל המציאות נחלקת עליהם. אכן כל שיש
בכלל כולו נוהג אפילו בפרט היותר קטן שבמציאות כנ"ל. ולמשל

example, even in the aspect of the Inanimate of the spiritual [World of] *Asiyah* (Action) alone it is possible to conceive there all five aspects: *Nefesh, Ruach, Neshamah, Chayah,* and *Yechidah,* which are related to the five aspects of *Nefesh, Ruach, Neshamah, Chayah,* and *Yechidah,* of the collective. In this sense, it is not possible to grasp even the Light of the Inanimate in [the World of] *Asiyah* unless it is through [the engagement in] the four parts of the work mentioned above.

It means that there is not one person among the Israelites who can absolve himself from engaging with all of them, according to his level. He must engage in the Torah and the Precepts with the proper *kavanah* (meditation) in order to receive the *Ruach* (Spirit) according to his level. And he must engage with the Secrets of the Torah according to his level in order to receive the aspect of *Neshamah* (Soul) according to his level. It is the same in the case of [engaging with] the Reasons [lit. taste] behind the Precepts because even the smallest Light in the Holy Reality cannot be made complete without them [the Secrets and Reasons].

אפילו בבחי' דומם דעשיה הרוחני בלבדו יש שם להשיג ה' בחינות נרנח"י נפש רוח נשמה חיה יחידה, שיש להם יחס לה' בחי' נרנח"י נפש רוח נשמה חיה יחידה הכוללים. באופן, שאי אפשר להשיג אפילו אור הדומם דעשיה, זולת ע"י על ידי ד' חלקי העבודה הנ"ל.

באופן, שאין לך אדם מישראל שיפטור עצמו מלעסוק בכולן, לפי ערכו, והוא צריך לעסוק בתורה ומצות בכונה בכדי לקבל בחי' רוח בערכו, והוא צריך לעסוק בסודות התורה לפי ערכו כדי שיקבל בחי' נשמה לפי ערכו, וכן בטעמי מצות, כי אי אפשר לאור היותר קטן שבמציאות הקדושה שיהיה נשלם זולתם.

Part Three:

Quantum Metaphysics

וזלק שליׁשי׳׳:

מטאפיׁזיקת הקוונטים

Chapter Eight: Who Let the Zohar Out?

Why does chaos get stronger in our time?

57) From this you will understand the barrenness and the darkness that have befallen us in this generation, the likes of which were not heard of in any generation prior to ours. This is because even those who work with the Creator have abandoned the engagement with the secrets of the Torah. The Rambam (Maimonides) came up with a true parable regarding this. He said that in a line of 1000 blind people walking along the road, if there is at least one sharp-sighted person at their head, they are all safe to go on the right path and not fall into any traps or nets because they are following the sharp-sighted person at their head. But missing that one [sharp-sighted] person, there is no doubt that they would stumble over everything lying in their way and would all fall into a pit of despair.

So this is the case before us: If at least those who work with the Creator would engage with the inner meaning of the Torah and [thereby] extend a complete Light from the *Ein Sof* (Endless), all the members of [our] generation would follow them, and all would be sure in their way that they would not fail. But when even those who work with the Creator have shied away from this wisdom, it is not surprising that the entire generation has failed because of them. However, because of my great sorrow, I cannot speak about this matter in greater length.

What was the "ladder" of Rav Ashlag?

58) However, I know the reason [for this failure]: It is mainly because [people's] trust (lit. faith) in general has declined, and in particular the trust in the supreme holy ones, the sages of the generations. Furthermore, the *Zohar* and [other] Kabbalah books are full with physical expressions, and that has caused great fear among everybody that they would lose rather than gain [by studying this], because, Heaven forbid, it may make them fail with the [first

פרק שמיני: מי כתב את הזוהר

מדוע מתגבר הכאוס בדורות שלנו?

נז) ומכאן תבין את היבשות והחשכות שמצאונו בדורנו זה שלא נשמע כמוהן בכל הדורות שקדמו לנו, שהוא משום שאפילו העובדי ה' שמטו ידיהם מהעסק בסודות התורה, וכבר המשיל הרמב"ם רבי משה בן מימון ז"ל משל אמיתי על זה, ואמר שאם שורה של אלף אנשים סומים הולכים בדרך, ויש להם לפחות פקח אחד בראשם הרי הם בטוחים כולם שילכו בדרך הישר, ולא יפלו בפחים ומכמורות, להיותם נמשכים אחר הפקח שבראשם. אבל אם חסר להם אותו האחד, בלי ספק שיכשלו בכל דבר המוטל בדרך, ויפלו כולם לבור שחת.

כן הדבר שלפנינו, אם היו לפחות עובדי השי"ת עוסקים בפנימיות התורה, והמשיכו אור שלם מא"ס ב"ה מאין סוף ברוך הוא, הרי כל בני הדור היו נמשכים אחריהם, וכולם היו בטוחים בדרכם שלא יכשלו, ואם גם עובדי השי"ת סלקו את עצמם מחכמה זו, אין פלא שכל הדור נכשל בגללם. ומגודל צערי, לא אוכל להאריך בזה.

מהו ה"סולם" של הרב אשלג?

נח) אמנם ידעתי הסבה, שהיא בעיקר מתוך שנתמעטה האמונה בכלל, והאמונה בקדושי עליון חכמי הדורות, בפרט, וספרי הקבלה והזהר מלאים ממשלים גשמיים, ע"כ על כן נפל הפחד על כל אחד,

Precept] about graven images. And this is what has motivated me to write a sufficient commentary on the writings of the Ari, Rav Isaac Luria, and now [a commentary] on the Holy *Zohar*, by which I have completely removed this fear.

As I have explained, and have clearly proven, the spiritual allegory of each subject, which is abstract beyond any physical resemblance, beyond time and space , as those who study will realize. [I have done] this to enable all the multitude of the Israelites to study the *Zohar* and to warm themselves in its Holy Light. And I have called this commentary the *Sulam* (Ladder) to show that the purpose of my commentary is just like any other ladder. If you have an attic that is full of all sorts of valuables, all that you are missing is a "ladder" to climb, and then [with a ladder,] the goodness of the whole world is in your hands.

But the ladder is not the goal in itself because if you rest on the steps of the ladder and do not enter the attic, then your purpose would not be achieved (lit. completed). So it is with my commentary on the *Zohar*. In order to explain their words, which are deeper than any depth, all the way to the end, expressions like this have not yet been created. In any case, in this explanation of mine, I have paved a road and opened a gate for every human being to be able to ascend through it and to go deeper and look at the *Zohar* itself, because only then will my purpose of creating this commentary be achieved (lit. completed).

Who really wrote the *Zohar*?

59) And all those who are familiar with the holy *Zohar*—that is to say, those who understand what is written in it—have unanimously agreed that the holy book of the *Zohar* was composed by the *Tanna* (divine sage of the Talmud), Rav Shimon bar Yochai. The exceptions to this are those who are distant from this wisdom, some of whom have doubts regarding this attribution. They tend to say, based on stories fabricated by those who oppose this wisdom, that its author is the kabbalist Rav Moshe de Leon [circa 1250-1305] or others of his contemporaries.

שלא יצא שכרו בהפסדו, כי ח"ו חס ושלום קרוב להכשל בפסל ודמות. והיא שהעירני לעשות ביאור, מספיק, על כהאר"י כתבי האר"י ז"ל, ועתה על הזהר הקדוש והסרתי הפחד הזה לגמרי.

כי ביארתי והוכחתי בעליל, את הנמשל הרוחני של כל דבר, שהוא מופשט מכל דמיון גשמי, למעלה מהמקום ולמעלה מהזמן, כמו שיראו המעיינים, למען לאפשר לכל המון בית ישראל ללמוד ספר הזהר, ולהתחמם באורו הקדוש. וקראתי הביאור בשם "הסולם" להורות, שתפקיד ביאורי הוא בתפקיד כל סולם, שאם יש לך עליה מלאה כל טוב, אינך חסר אלא "סולם" לעלות בו, ואז כל טוב העולם בידך.

אמנם אין "הסולם" מטרה כלפי עצמו: כי אם תנוח במדרגות הסולם ולא תכנס אל העליה, אז לא תושלם כונתך. כן הדבר בביאור שלי על הזוהר, כי לבאר דבריהם, העמוקים מכל עמוק, עד סופם. עוד לא נברא הביטוי לזה, אלא עשיתי על כל פנים בביאורי זה, דרך ומבוא לכל בן אדם שיוכל על ידו לעלות ולהעמיק ולהסתכל בספר הזהר גופו, כי רק אז, תושלם כונתי בביאורי זה.

מי באמת חיבר את ספר הזוהר?

נט) והנה כל המצוים אצל ספר הזהר הקדוש, כלומר, המבינים מה שכתוב בו, הסכימו פה אחד, שספר הזהר הקדוש חיברו, התנא האלקי, רבי שמעון בן יוחאי. חוץ מהרחוקים מחכמה זו, ושיש מהם המפקפקים ביחוסו זה, ונוטים לומר, על סמך מעשיות בדויות ממתנגדי החכמה הזו, שמחברו הוא, המקובל ר' משה די ליאון, או אחרים הסמוכים לו בזמן.

149

60) As for myself, from the day that I merited, by the Light of the Creator, to glance briefly into this sacred book, it did not even occur to me to question its origin. This is for the very simple reason that because of the content of the book, I felt in my heart the greatness of the Tanna, Rav Shimon bar Yochai, that has risen way above all the other holy *Tanna* sages. And had it become completely clear to me that the author [of the *Zohar*] had a different name, such as Rav Moshe de Leon, etc., then my appreciation for that man, Rav Moshe de Leon, would have grown to be more than my appreciation of all the holy *Tanna* sages, including Rav Shimon bar Yochai.

Truly, because of the depth of the wisdom in the book, had I found clear evidence that its author was one of the 48 prophets, this would have been much easier for me to accept in my heart than attributing it to one of the *Tanna* sages. And even more so, had I found that our great Master, Moses, had received [the *Zohar*] on Mount Sinai from the Creator Himself, then my mind would have been completely at rest because such a piece is worthy of Him [the Creator] and it behooves Him to have created it.

Therefore, because I had the privilege of writing an appropriate explanation that is on the level of anyone interested in study, so that they are able to understand somewhat the content of the book, I think that in this I have been completely exempt from bothering further and putting myself into this question, because anyone who has studied the *Zohar* can no longer have doubt in the assumption that its author is anyone less than the Tanna, Rav Shimon bar Yochai.

Why was the *Zohar* not revealed to earlier generations?

61) This brings up another question: Why was this book [the *Zohar*] not revealed to the first generations, which were undoubtedly of higher significance than the more recent generations [our generation] and were more worthy of [such a revelation]? At the same time, we

ס) ואני כשאני לעצמי, הרי מיום שזכיתי באור השי"ת להתבונן מעט בספר הקדוש הזה לא עלה על לבי לחקור ביחוסו, והוא מטעם פשוט, כי לפי תוכנו של הספר, עלה בלבי מעלת יקר התנא רשב"י, לאין ערך יותר על כל התנאים הקדושים, ואם היה מתברר לי בבירור גמור שמחברו הוא שם אחר, כגון ר"מ רבי משה די ליאון ז"ל, וכדומה, הרי אז, היה גדל אצלי מעלת האיש ר"מ רבי משה די ליאון ז"ל יותר מכל התנאים הקדושים, וגם רשב"י רבי שמעון בר יוחאי בכללם.

אמנם באמת לפי מדת עומק החכמה שבספר, אם הייתי מוצא בבירור, שמחברו הוא אחד ממ"ח הנביאים, היה זה מקובל על לבי ביותר, מליחסו לאחד מהתנאים, ומכ"ש ומכל שכן אם הייתי מוצא, שמשה רבינו קבל אותו מהר סיני מהשי"ת מהשם יתברך עצמו, אז היתה שוככת דעתי לגמרי, כי לו נאה ולו יאה חיבור כזה.

ולפיכך כיון שזכיתי לערוך ביאור מספיק השוה לכל בעל עיון, להבין מעט מה שכתוב בו בספר, אני חושב שכבר נפטרתי בזה לגמרי מלטרוח עוד ולהכניס עצמי בחקירה הזאת, כי כל משכיל בזהר לא יוכל להסתפק עוד, שמחברו יוכל להיות איש פחות במעלה מהתנא רשב"י רבי שמעון בר יוחאי הקדוש.

למה לא נגלה הזוהר לדורות ראשונים?

סא) אכן לפי"ז לפי זה נשאלת השאלה, למה לא היה נגלה ספר הזהר לדורות הראשונים, שבלי ספק היו חשובים במעלה יותר מדורות האחרונים והיו ראויים לו יותר, ויחד עם זה יש לשאול למה לא נגלה ביאור ספר הזהר עד האריז"ל, ולא למקובלים

have to ask: Why was the explanation of this book not revealed until the time of Rav Isaac Luria and not to the kabbalists who came before him? And the question that surpasses all other questions: Why was the explanation of the words of the Ari, as well as the words of the *Zohar* from the days of the Ari, not revealed until our present generation? (Study my introduction to the book *Panim Masbirot* (Pleasant Face) about the Tree of Life in verse 8, starting with the words: "And it is written "… Study this well.)

This raises the question: Is our generation fit for this [revelation]? And the answer is that the world, during the 6000 years of existance, is like one *Partzuf* (Spiritual Structure), which has three thirds: the head, the middle, and the end, that is to say, *Chochmah* (Wisdom), *Binah* (Understanding), *Da'at* (Knowledge) [head]; *Chesed* (Mercy), *Gevurah* (Judgment), *Tiferet* (Splendor) [middle]; *Netzach* (Eternity), *Hod* (Glory), and *Yesod* (Foundation) [end]. And this is what our sages said: Two thousand years of chaos; two thousand years of Torah; and two thousand years of the days of the Messiah. (Tractate *Sanhedrin* 97a). Because in the first 2000 [years], which are referred to as the Head and [comprise of] *Chochmah*, *Binah* and *Da'at*, the Lights were very few and were considered to be a Head without a Body, which only has the Lights of *Nefesh* (Lower Soul).

This is because there is an inverse relationship between Vessels and Lights. For in the Vessels, the rule is that the first Vessels grow at first in each *Partzuf* (Spiritual Structure), and with regards to the Lights, it is the other way round: The lower Lights are enclothed with the *Partzuf* at first. And so it turns out that as long as the Vessels are only the higher, namely the Vessels of *Chochmah* (Wisdom), *Binah* (Understanding), *Da'at* (Knowledge), they become the cloth of the Lights of *Nefesh* (Lower Soul) only, which are the most inferior Lights.

And this is what is meant when it says that the first 2000 years are [the years of] *Tohu* (Chaos). And in the second 2000 years of the world, which are the aspect of *Chesed* (Mercy), *Gevurah* (Judgment), *Tiferet* (Splendor) of the Vessels, the Light of *Ruach*

שקדמו לו. וההתמיה העולה על כולנה, למה לא נגלו ביאור דברי האריז"ל, ודברי הזוהר מימי האריז"ל עד דורנו זו (וע" בהקדמתי לספר פנים מסבירות על הע"ח העץ חיים באות ח' ד"ה ואיתא עש"ה דבור המתחיל [במילה] ואיתא, עיין שם היטב).

ונשאלת השאלה, הכי אכשר דרי האם הדור שלנו מוכן. והתשובה היא, כי העולם, במשך זמן קיומו של שתא אלפי שני ששת אלפים שנה, הוא כמו פרצוף אחד, שיש לו ג' שלישים ראש תוך וסוף, דהיינו חב"ד חכמה בינה ודעת, חג"ת חסד גבורה תפארת, נה"י נצח הוד יסוד. וז"ש ז"ל וזה שאמרו [רבותינו] זכרונם לברכה: ב' אלפים תהו, ב' אלפים תורה, וב' אלפים ימות המשיח (מסכת סנהדרין דף צז, עמוד מ"א) כי בב' אלפים הראשונים שהם בחינת ראש וחב"ד חכמה בינה דעת, היו האורות מועטים מאוד, והיו נחשבים לבחינת ראש בלי גוף, שאין בו אלא אורות דנפש.

כי יש ערך הפוך בין כלים לאורות, כי בכלים, הכלל הוא, שהכלים הראשונים נגדלים בכל פרצוף מתחילה, ובאורות הוא להיפך, שאורות התחתונים מתלבשים בפרצוף מתחילה, ונמצא כל עוד שאין בכלים רק העליונים לבד, דהיינו כלים דחב"ד של חכמה בינה דעת, יורדים שם להתלבש רק אורות דנפש, שהם האורות התחתונים ביותר.

וז"ש וזה שכתוב על ב' אלפים ראשונים שהם בבחינת תהו. ובב' אלפים השניים של העולם, שהם בחינת חג"ת חסד גבורה תפארת דכלים, ירד ונתלבש אור הרוח בעולם, שה"ס שהוא סוד תורה. וע"כ ועל כן אמרו על

(Spirit) descended and enclothed itself in the world, [and that Light of *Ruach*] is the secret of Torah. And therefore [the sages] said that the middle 2000 years are [the years of] Torah. And the last 2000 years are *Netzach* (Eternity), *Hod* (Glory), *Yesod* (Foundation), and *Malchut* (Kingdom) of the Vessels, and therefore at that time the Light of *Neshamah* (Soul) is clothed in this world. [This Light of *Neshamah*] is the greatest Light, and therefore these [last 2000 years] are the days of the Messiah.

This is also the way it works regarding each individual *Partzuf* (Spiritual Structure). Thus, in the Vessels of *Chochmah* (Wisdom), *Binah* (Understanding), *Da'at* (Knowledge), *Chesed* (Mercy), *Gevurah* (Judgment), *Tiferet* (Splendor), which come up to his [the *Partzuf*] Chest, the Lights are veiled and they don't start shining the revealed [Light of] *Chasadim* (Mercies)—that is, the revelation of the illumination of the Supernal [Light of] *Chochmah* (Wisdom)—but only from the Chest downwards; that is to say, in his *Netzach* (Eternity), *Hod* (Glory), *Yesod* (Foundation), and *Malchut* (Kingdom). And this is the reason that before the Vessels of *Netzach, Hod, Yesod,* and *Malchut* started to appear in the *Partzuf* of the World, which refers to the last 2000 years, the Wisdom of the *Zohar* in general and the Wisdom of Kabbalah in particular were concealed from the world.

Why was the Ari chosen to inaugurate the Era of Redemption?

But during the time of the Ari (Rav Isaac Luria) when the time of completion of the Vessels that are from the Chest Downwards was drawing near, then the illumination of the Sublime wisdom was revealed in a concealed manner by the soul of the divine Rav Isaac Luria, who was ready to receive this great Light. And therefore he revealed the principles of the Book of the *Zohar* and also the Wisdom of Kabbalah to the point that he overshadowed all the

ב' אלפים האמצעים שהם תורה. וב' אלפים האחרונים הם נהי"מ נצח, הוד, יסוד, מלכות דכלים וע"כ ועל כן מתלבש בעולם בזמן ההוא אור דנשמה. שהוא האור היותר גדול, וע"כ ועל כן הם ימות המשיח.

גם הדרך הוא בכל פרצוף פרטי, שבכלים דחב"ד של חכמה בינה דעת חג"ת חסד גבורה תפארת עד החזה שלו, האורות מכוסים, ואינם מתחילים להאיר חסדים המגולים, שפירושו, התגלות הארת חכמה עליונה, אלא מחזה ולמטה, דהיינו בנהי"מ בנצח הוד יסוד ומלכות שלו. והוא הסבה, שמטרם התחילו להתגלות הכלים דנהי"מ של נצח הוד יסוד ומלכות בפרצוף העולם, שהם ב' אלפים האחרונים, היתה חכמה הזהר בכלל וחכמת הקבלה בפרט, מכוסה מן העולם.

מדוע התגלה האר"י דווקא בימות משיח?

אלא בזמן האריז"ל שכבר נתקרב זמן השלמת הכלים שמחזה ולמטה, נתגלתה אז הארת חכמה העליונה בהעלם, ע"י על ידי נשמת האלקי ר' יצחק לוריא ז"ל, שהיה מוכן לקבל האור הגדול הזה, וע"כ ועל כן גילה העיקרים שבספר הזהר, וגם חכמת הקבלה, עד שהעמיד

Rishonim (Firsts) who preceded him. However since these Vessels were not fully completed yet (for he passed on in the year 5332 [1572 AD], as is known), therefore the world was not yet worthy for his words to be revealed.

And his [the Ari's] holy words were given only to a select few, and [these few] were not given permission to reveal them to the world. And now in this generation of ours, since we are very near the end of the last 2000 years, the permission has therefore now been granted to reveal [both] his words and the words of the *Zohar* to the world, to a great and important extent. In this way, from this generation of ours onwards, the words of the *Zohar* will be made more and more revealed until the full and complete extent will be revealed according to the will of the Creator

Why our spiritually low generations will reveal the greatest Light ever?

63) And therefore you will understand that in truth, there is no end to the degree of the greatness of the first generations over the recent ones. This is the rule with regard to all the *Partzufim* (Spiritual Structures) of the Worlds and [all] the souls: That which is which is pristine is purified first into the *Partzuf*. And therefore, the Vessels of *Chochmah* (Wisdom), *Binah* (Understanding), and *Da'at* (Knowledge) were purified first in the World and from the souls too, and therefore the souls in the first 2000 years were endlessly superior.

Even so, they were not able to achieve the stature of full Light because the lower parts [vessels] were missing from the World and from themselves; these [low vessels] are *Chesed* (Mercy), *Gevurah* (Judgment), *Tiferet* (Splendor), *Netzach* (Eternity), *Hod* (Glory), *Yesod* (Foundation), and *Malchut* (Kingdom), as mentioned above. And also later, in the middle 2000 years--when the vessels of *Chesed*, *Gevurah*, and *Tiferet* were refined into the World and in the souls--the souls from their own aspect were actually still extremely pure. Because the quality of the Vessels of *Chesed*, *Gevurah*, and *Tiferet*

בצד, כל הראשונים שקדמוהו. ועכ"ז ועם כל זה כיון שהכלים האלו עוד לא נשלמו לגמרי (שהוא נפטר בזמן ה' אלפים של"ב כנודע.) ע"כ על כן לא היה העולם עוד ראוי שיתגלו דבריו.

ולא היו דבריו הקדושים, אלא קנין ליחידי סגולה מועטים. שלא ניתנה להם הרשות לגלותם בעולם. וכעת בדורנו זה, אחר שכבר קרובים אנו, לגמר ב' אלפים האחרונים, לפיכך ניתנה עתה הרשות לגלות דבריו ז"ל, ודברי הזהר בעולם, בשיעור חשוב מאד. באופן שמדורנו זה ואילך יתחילו להתגלות דברי הזהר בכל פעם יותר ויותר, עד שיתגלה כל השיעור השלם שבחפץ השי"ת.

מדוע הדורות הנמוכים שלנו יגלו דווקא את האור הגדול ?

סג) ולפי"ז ולפי זה תבין שבאמת אין קץ לשיעור מעלתם של דורות הראשונים על האחרונים, כי זה הכלל בכל הפרצופין של העולמות ושל הנשמות, אשר כל הזך נברר תחילה אל הפרצוף ולפיכך נבררו תחילה הכלים דחב"ד של חכמה בינה דעת מהעולם וכן מהנשמות, ולפיכך היו הנשמות שבב' אלפים הראשונים גבוהות לאין קץ.

ועכ"ז ועם כל זה לא יכלו לקבל קומת אור שלם, מפאת החסרון של החלקים הנמוכים מהעולם ומהן עצמן, שהם חג"ת חסד גבורה תפארת נהי"מ נצח הוד יסוד ומלכות כנ"ל. וכן אח"כ אחר כך בב' אלפים האמצעים, שנתבררו הכלים דחג"ת של חסד גבורה תפארת אל העולם וכן מן הנשמות, היו הנשמות באמת מבחינת עצמן עוד זכות עד מאוד כי כלים דחג"ת של חסד גבורה תפארת מעלתם קרובה לחב"ד חכמה בינה

is very close [in its purity] to that of *Chochmah* (Wisdom), *Binah* (Understanding) and *Da'at* (Knowledge) (as is mentioned in the *Zohar*, Prologue, page 11, starting with the words: "And what..."). And yet the Lights were still concealed in the world because the Vessels from the Chest Down were missing from the world and also from the souls.

Consequently, in our generation, even though the essence of the souls is the worst[2] that could be, which is why they could not be refined to holiness until this day, still they are the ones who complete the *Partzuf* (Spiritual Structure) of the world and the *Partzuf* of the entirety of the souls, as far as the Vessels are concerned and the work can be completed only by them.

Because now that the Vessels of *Netzach* (Eternity), *Hod* (Glory), and *Yesod* (Foundation) are completed, and now that we have all the Vessels: Head (beginning), Middle, and End of the Partzuf, all the complete statures of Lights in the Head, Middle, and End, are drawn to all those who are worthy of them, namely the complete *Nefesh* (Lower Soul), *Ruach* (Spirit), and *Neshamah* (Soul) as was mentioned earlier. And therefore, only with the completion of these lower souls can the higher Lights be revealed, and not before that.

64) In truth, this query already exists in the words of the sages (in Tractate *Brachot*, page 20a). Rav Papa said to [Rav] Abayey: "What was different about earlier [generations] for whom miracles occurred and what is different about us for whom miracles do not occur? Is it because of their [superiority in] study? Because in the time of Rav Yehudah, the entirety of their studies was confined to [the Tractate] *Nezikin*, and we study all six Tractates (of the *Mishnah*), and when Rav Yehudah came in [the Tractate] *Ukzin* [to the law]...he used to say, I see here all the difficulties of Rav and Samuel. Whereas we study [nowadays] thirteen [different] versions of [Tractate] *Ukzin*

---

2   Lowest level, poor quality, coarse

דעת, (כמ"ש בהקסה"ז די"א ד"ה כמו שכתוב בהקדמת ספר הזוהר, דף יא דבור המתחיל [במילה] ומה) **ועכ"ז** ועם כל זה **עוד היו האורות מכוסים בעולם, מטעם חסרון הכלים, שמחזה ולמטה מהעולם, וכן מן הנשמות.**

ולפיכך בדורנו זה, שהגם שמהות הנשמות. הללו היא הגרועה שבמציאות, כי ע"כ על כן **לא יכלו להתברר לקדושה עד היום, עם זה המה המשלימים את פרצוף העולם ופרצוף כללות הנשמות, מבחינת הכלים, ואין המלאכה נשלמת אלא על ידיהם,**

כי עתה כשכבר נשלמים הכלים דנה"י של נצח הוד יסוד**, ויש עתה כל הכלים ראש תוך וסוף בפרצוף, נמשכים עתה קומות שלימות של האורות, בראש תוך וסוף, לכל הכדאים להם, דהיינו נר"**ן נפש רוח נשמה שלמים**, כנ"ל. ולפיכך רק עם השתלמותן של הנשמות הנמוכות הללו, יכולים האורות העליונים להתגלות ולא מקודם לכן.**

סד) ובאמת נמצאת קושיא זו עוד בדברי חז"ל (במס' ברכות דף כ' ע"א) **אמר ליה** אמר לו **רב פפא לאביי, מאי שנא ראשונים דאתרחיש להו ניסא** במה שונים [הדורות] הראשונים שהתרחשו להם ניסים**, מאי שנא אנן דלא מתרחיש להו ניסא** ובמה שונים אנו שלא מתרחשים לנו ניסים**? אי משום תנויי, בשני דרב יהודה כולי תנויי בנזיקין הוה** אם משום הלימוד: בשנותיו של רב יהודה כל למודם היה רק [בסדר] נזיקין**, ואנן קא מתנינן שיתא סדרי** ואנחנו לומדים כל ששת סדרי [משנה] **וכי הוה מטי רב יהודה בעוקצין וכו'** וכאשר היה מגיע רב יהודה [במסכת] עוקצין וכו' **אמר הויות דרב ושמאל קא חזינא הכא** [היה מתקשה] ואומר: את מחלוקת רב ושמואל אני רואה כאן**, ואנן קא מתנינן בעוקצין תליסר מתיבתא** ואנחנו לומדים [במסכת] עוקצין בשלוש עשרה נוסחאות [שונות]**. ואלו רב יהודה כד הוה שליף חד מסאניה אתי מטרא** ואלו

and yet when [there was drought] Rav Yehudah would merely remove one shoe, rain would fall immediately. Whereas we afflict ourselves and cry loudly (in prayers), and no one pays attention to us!' [Abayey] replied: The earlier [generations] used to be ready to sacrifice their lives for the sanctity of [the Creator's] Name ect. " End of quote, Study this well.

Thus, even though both he who questioned and he who answered were very clear that the earlier [generations] were more important than them, still, as far as the Torah and the Wisdom [of Kabbalah] were concerned, Rav Papa and [Rav] Abayey were more important than the *Rishonim* (earlier sages). It is clear that even though the earlier generations were more important than the later generations as far as the essence of their soul as mentioned above, because the pristine is purified first to come to [this] World, still, the wisdom of the Torah is becoming revealed more and more in the later generations. This is because of what we have said [above]: that because the general stature is actually being completed specifically by the later [generations], therefore more complete Lights are being extended to them, even though their own essence is extremely worse[3].

What did the first generations know about Kabbalah?

65) And we should not question, based on this, why it is forbidden to dispute with the earlier [generations] regarding the Revealed Torah. The point is that as far as completing the action (ceremonial) part of the Precepts is the opposite, because the earlier [generations] were more complete in them [the actions of the Precepts] than the more recent ones. This is because the aspect of the action extends from the holy Vessels of the *Sefirot*, while the Secrets of the Torah and the reasons behind the Precepts extend from the Lights of the *Sefirot*.

---

3   Lowest level, poor quality, coarse

[בשעת תענית על המטר] כאשר רב יהודה היה שולף נעלו האחת מיד היה יורד הגשם, **ואנן קא מצערינן נפשין ומצווח קא צווחינן ולית דמשגח בן ואנחנו מצערים** את עצמנו וצווחים ואין משגיח בנו. **אמר ליה קמאי הוו קא מסרי נפשייהו אקדושת השם וכו'** אמר לו [אביי] הראשונים היו מוסרים את נפשם על קדושת השם וכו' **עכ"ל** עד כאן לשונו **עש"ה** עיין שם היטב.

הרי שאע"פ שאף על פי שהן למקשן והן למתרץ, היה ברור שהראשונים היו חשובים מהם, מ"מ מכל מקום מבחינת התורה והחכמה, היו רב פפא ואביי יותר חשובים מהראשונים. הרי מפורש, שאע"פ שאף על פי שהדורות הראשונים חשובים יותר מדורות האחרונים במהות נשמתם עצמם כנ"ל, שהוא מטעם שכל הזך ביותר נברר תחילה לבוא לעולם, מ"מ מבחי' מכל מקום מבחינת חכמת התורה היא מתגלית יותר ויותר בדורות אחרונים. והוא מטעם שאמרנו, כי מתוך שקומה הכללית, הולכת ונשלמת על ידי היותר אחרונים דוקא, לכן נמשכים להם אורות יותר שלמים אע"פ ואף על פי שמהותם עצמם הוא גרועה ביותר.

מה ידעו דורות ראשונים על חכמת הנסתר?

סה) ואין להקשות לפי"ז לפי זה, א"כ אם כן למה אסור, לחלוק על הראשונים בתורת הנגלה. הענין הוא כי במה ששייך להשלמת חלק המעשי מהמצות, הוא להיפך, שהראשונים נשלמו בהם יותר מהאחרונים והוא משום שבבחינת המעשה, נמשכת מהכלים הקדושים של הספירות, וסודות התורה וטעמי המצוה נמשכים מהאורות שבספירות.

As we already know, there is an inverse relationship between the Vessels and the Lights: In the Vessels, the higher ones grow first (as we have mentioned above in verse 62), which is why the *Rishonim* (earlier sages) were perfected with regard to practicing [the Precepts] than the later [generations]. This is not so with regard to the Lights, where the lower ones enter first, and therefore the lower ones [later generations] are more complete with them [that is the Lights] than the *Rishonim* (earlier sages). Understand this well!

וכבר ידעת שיש ערך הפוך מהכלים להאורות, שבכלים, העליונים
נגדלים מתחילה, (כנ"ל אות ס"ב) וע"כ ועל כן נשלמו הראשונים
בחלק המעשה יותר מהאחרונים. משא"כ מה שאין כן באורות,
שהתחתונים נכנסים מתחילה. וע"כ ועל כן נשלמים בהם התחתונים
יותר מהראשונים. והבן היטב.

Chapter Nine: The Internet of the Souls

What is the inner and exterior aspect of the world?

66) You should know that everything has an inner aspect and an exterior one. In the totality of the world the Israelites—the descendants of Abraham, Isaac, and Jacob—are considered the interiority of the world, and the 70 nations are considered the exteriority of the world. And also among the Israelites there is the interiority, which are those who fully perform the work with the Creator, and the exteriority, which are those who are not devoted to the work with the Creator. Similarly, among the [70] Nations of the World, there is the interiority, which are the Righteous from the Nations, and the exteriority, which is the vulgar and harmful in them, etc.

Even among the Israelites who work with the Creator, there is the interiority, which are those who merit understanding the soul of the interiority of the Torah and its secrets, and the exteriority, which are those who deal only with the practicing part of the Torah. And in the same way, every person of the Israelites has interiority, which is the aspect of Israel in him, which is the secret of the Point in the Heart. And there is also an exteriority, which is the aspect of the Nations of the World in him which is the body itself. But even the aspect of the Nations of the World in him [the body] is considered as proselytes; since [the body parts] are attached to the interiority [the Point of the Heart], they are like the righteous proselytes from the Nations of the World who came and attached themselves to the Israelites.

How to strengthen our inner power?

67) And when a person of the Israelite enhances and dignifies the aspect of his interiority, which is the aspect of the Israelite within him, over his exteriority, which is the aspect of the Nations of the World in him—that is to say, when he expends most of his effort

פרק תשיעי: האינטרנט של הנשמות

מהי הפנימיות והחצוניות של העולם?

סו) ודע, שבכל דבר יש פנימיות וחיצוניות, ובכללות העולם נחשבים ישראל, זרע אברהם יצחק ויעקב, לפנימיות העולם, וע' 70 אומות, נחשבים לחיצוניות העולם. וכן בישראל עצמם יש פנימיות, שהם עובדי השי"ת השלמים, וכן יש חיצוניות, שאינם מתמסרים לעבודת השי"ת. וכן באומות העולם עצמם, יש פנימיות, שהם חסידי אומות העולם, ויש חיצוניות שהם הגסים והמזיקים שבהם וכדומה.

וכן בעובדי השי"ת השם יתברך שבבני ישראל, יש פנימיות, שהם הזוכים להבין נשמת פנימיות התורה וסודותיה, וחיצוניות שהם אותם שאינם עוסקים אלא בחלק המעשה שבתורה. וכן בכל אדם מישראל, יש בו פנימיות, שהיא בחינת ישראל שבו, שה"ס שהוא סוד הנקודה שבלב. וחיצוניות, שהיא בחינת אוה"ע אומות העולם שבו, שהוא הגוף עצמו. אלא שאפילו בחי' אוה"ע בחינת אומות העולם שבו נחשבים בו כמו גרים. כי להיותם דבוקים על הפנימיות, הם דומים לגרי צדק מאומות העולם, שבאו והתדבקו בכלל ישראל.

כיצד לחזק את כח הפנימיות?

סז) ובהיות האדם מישראל, מגביר ומכבד את בחינת פנימיותו, שהיא בחינת ישראל שבו, על חיצוניותו, שהיא בחינת אוה"ע אומות העולם שבו דהיינו שנותן רוב טרחתו ויגיעתו להגדיל ולהעלות בחינת

and his labor to increase and to raise the aspect of interiority within him for the benefit of his soul, and [expends] little effort, only to the necessary degree, to the existence of the Nations of the World aspect within him, that is, for the bodily needs, as was said (in the *Pirkei Avot* (Ethics of the Fathers): "Make your Torah permanent and your work temporary." Thus, through his actions in both the interiority and the exteriority of the whole world, he causes the Israelites to keep on increasing in their perfection higher and higher, so that the Nations of the World, which represent the exteriority of the world at large, will recognize and appreciate the value of the Israelites.

And if, Heaven forbid, the opposite happens—that an individual from Israel emphasizes and gives more importance to the aspect of his exteriority, which is the aspect of the Nations of the World within him, over the aspect of Israelite within him—then, as is said: "The strange who is among you" (Deuteronomy 28:43) that is, the exteriority within you, "shall mount above you higher and higher; and you…" yourself, that is to say, your interiority, which is the aspect of the Israelite in you, "…shall go down lower and lower."

And thus, through his actions, he causes the exteriority of the world in general, which is the Nations of the World, to rise up higher and higher, and overcome the Israelites and humiliate them to the ground; and the Israelites, who are the interiority of the world, [then] go down lower and lower, Heaven forbid.

How can everything be connected to everything?

68) And it should not surprise you that an individual can, through his own actions, cause any rise or decline to the whole world. It is an immutable law that the collective and the individual are equal to each other like two drops of water, and everything that applies to the collective also applies to the individual. [This being said], it is [actually] the individuals who make the collective do what it does. This is because the collective will be realized [as a collective]

פנימיות שבו לתועלת נפשו, וטרחה מועטת בשיעור המוכרח הוא
נותן לקיום בחי' אוה"ע בחינת אומות העולם שבו, דהיינו לצרכי הגוף.
דהיינו כמ"ש כמו שכתוב (פרקי אבות פ"א פרק א') עשה תורתך קבע
ומלאכתך עראי. הנה אז גורם במעשיו, גם בפו"ח בפנימיות וחצוניות
דכללות העולם, שבני ישראל עולים בשלמותם מעלה מעלה,
ואוה"ע ואומות העולם, שהם החיצוניות שבכללות, יכירו ויחשיבו את
ערך בני ישראל.

ואם ח"ו חס ושלום להיפך שהאדם הפרטי מישראל, מגביר ומחשיב
את בחינת חיצוניותו, שהיא בחינת אוה"ע אומות העולם שבו, על בחינת
ישראל שבו, וכמ"ש כמו שכתוב (דברים כ"ח) "הגר אשר בקרבך",
דהיינו החיצוניות שבו, "יעלה עליך מעלה מעלה, ואתה", בעצמך,
דהיינו הפנימיות, שהיא בחינת ישראל שבך, "תרד מטה מטה".

אז גורם במעשיו, שגם החיצוניות שבכללות העולם, שהם אוה"ע
אומות העולם, עולים מעלה מעלה, ומתגברים על ישראל ומשפילים
אותם עד לעפר, ובני ישראל, שהם הפנימיות שבעולם ירדו מטה
מטה ח"ו חס ושלום.

איך יכול אדם בודד להשפיע על כל העולם?

סח) ואל תתמה על זה, שאדם פרטי יגרום במעשיו מעלה או ירידה
לכל העולם. כי זהו חוק ולא יעבור, אשר הכלל והפרט כב' טפות
מים, וכל שנוהג בכלל כולו נוהג גם בפרט, ואדרבה, הפרטים

only after the individuals within [it] have manifested themselves, according to the quantity and quality of the individuals. So surely [it is] the action of the individual, according to its value, [that] causes the whole collective to either rise or decline.

By this, it will be clear to you what we have learned in the *Zohar*: that out of engagement with the *Zohar* and with the Wisdom of Truth, they shall merit coming out of exile into complete redemption [*Tikkunei* (Corrections to the) *Zohar*, End of Correction 6]. Seemingly, [one might ask] what is the connection between studying the *Zohar* and the redemption of the Israelites from among the nations?

What is the power that changes the world for better or worse?

69) By what has been explained, it is clearly understood that even the Torah has interiority and and exteriority, just like the world as a whole. Therefore, [it follows that] a person who is engaged with the Torah has also these two aspects. And as he increases his effort in the interior aspect of the Torah and its secrets, then to that same degree he causes the quality of the interiority of the world, which is the Israelites, to keep on ascending and rising higher above the exteriority of the world, that is, the Nations of the World [until eventually] all the nations will agree and recognize the quality of the Israelites over them, to the point where the [following] scriptural passages would be fulfilled: "And the nations will take them [the Israelites] and bring them to their place, and they will settle the House of Israel in the land of the Lord," etc. (Isaiah 14:2), as well as the following passage: "Thus said the Lord: Behold, I will lift up My hand to the nations, and raise My signal to the peoples; and they shall bring your sons in their bosom, and your daughters shall be carried on their shoulders." (Isaiah 49:22)

But if, Heaven forbid, the opposite [should happen], that the person from the Israelites would degrade the importance of the interiority of the Torah and its secrets, which deals with the ways of our souls and their levels as well as with our mind and the reasoning (also

עושים כל מה שבכלל כולו. כי לא יתגלה הכלל אלא לאחר גילוי הפרטים שבו, ולפי מדתם ואיכותם של הפרטים. וודאי שמעשה הפרט לפי ערכו מוריד או מעלה את הכלל כולו.

ובזה יתבאר לך מה שאיתא בזהר, שמתוך העסק בספר הזהר ובחכמת האמת, יזכו לצאת מתוך הגלות לגאולה שלימה. (תיקונים סוף תק' ו') שלכאורה, מה ענין לימוד הזוהר לגאולתם של ישראל מבין האומות.

מי מניע את העולם כולו לטוב ולרע?

סט) ובהמבואר מובן היטב, כי גם התורה יש בה פו"ח פנימיות וחיצוניות כמו כללות העולם כולו, ולפיכך גם העוסק בתורה, יש לו אלו ב' המדרגות. ובהיותו מגביר טרחתו בפנימיות התורה וסודותיה, נמצא גורם בשיעור הזה שמעלת פנימיות העולם, שהם ישראל, תעלה מעלה מעלה על חיצוניות העולם, שהם אוה"ע אומות העולם, וכל האומות יודו ויכירו בשבחם של ישראל עליהם, עד שיקוים הכתוב (ישעיה י"ד) ולקחום עמים והביאום אל מקומם, והתנחלום בית ישראל על אדמת ה' וגו'. וכמו כן הכתוב (ישעיה כ"ב) כה אמר ה' אלקים, הנה אשא אל גויים ידי, ואל עמים ארים נסי והביאו בניך בחוצן, ובנותיך על כתף תנשאנה.

אבל אם ח"ו חס ושלום להיפך, שהאדם מישראל, משפיל מעלת פנימיות התורה וסודותיה, הדנה בדרכי נשמותינו ומדרגותיהן, וכן בחלק השכל וטעמי מצוה, כלפי מעלת חיצוניות התורה הדנה

taste) behind each of the Precepts, in favor of praising the virtue of the exteriority of the Torah, which deals only with the practicing aspects—and even if he does engage with the interiority of the Torah, but he devotes to it only a small portion of his time, during a time that is neither day nor night, as if it [the interiority of the Torah] were, Heaven forbid, something that has no value—in this, that person is causing the interiority of the world, which are the Israelites, to go down lower and lower, and he makes the exteriority of the world, which is the Nations of the World, stronger and stronger so that they [eventually] humiliate the Israelites and put them to shame, and consider the Israelites as something superfluous in the world and that the world has no need for, Heaven forbid.

Moreover, through this [action], they even cause the exteriority of the Nations of the World to grow in strength over their own interiority because the worst of the Nations of the World, which are the evildoers and the destroyers of the world, grow stronger and rise higher and higher over their interiority, which is the Righteous from among the Nations of the World. And then they commit all their horrendous destruction and slaying, which the people of our generation have witnessed—may the Creator protect us from here onwards.

This demonstrates to you that [both] the redemption and all the virtue of the Israelites depend on the study of the *Zohar* and the interiority of the Torah. On the other hand, all the destruction and all the decline of the Israelites has happened because they have neglected the interiority of the Torah and have degraded its virtue lower and lower and have turned it, Heaven forbid, into something that is not needed at all.

בחלק המעשה בלבד - ואפילו אם עוסק פעם בפנימיות התורה, הריהו מקציב לה שעה מועטת מזמנו, בשעה שלא יום ולא לילה, כמו שהיתה ח"ו חס ושלום, דבר שאין צורך בו - הוא נמצא גורם בזה, להשפיל ולהוריד מטה מטה את פנימיות העולם, שהם בני ישראל, ולהגביר את חיצוניות העולם עליהם, שהם אוה"ע אומות העולם, וישפילו ויבזו את בני ישראל, ויחשיבו את ישראל כמו שהיו דבר מיותר בעולם. ואין לעולם חפץ בהם ח"ו חס ושלום.

ולא עוד, אלא גורמים בזה, שאפילו החיצוניות שבאוה"ע שבאומות העולם מתגברת על פנימיות שלהן עצמן, כי הגרועים שבאוה"ע שבאומות העולם, שהם המזיקים ומחריבי העולם, מתגברים ועולים מעלה מעלה על הפנימיות שלהם, שהם חסידי אומה"ע אומות העולם, ואז הם עושים כל החורבנות והשחיטות האיומים, שבני דורנו היו עדי ראיה להם, השם ישמרנו מכאן ואילך.

הרי לעיניך, שגאולת ישראל וכל מעלת ישראל, תלוי בלימוד הזוהר ובפנימיות התורה, ולהיפך, כל החורבנות וכל ירידתם של בני ישראל, הם מחמת שעזבו את פנימיות התורה, והשפילו מעלתה מטה מטה, ועשו אותה כמו שהיתה ח"ו חס ושלום דבר שאין צורך בו כלל.

Who really is responsible for all the chaos, pain and suffering in the world?

70) And this is what was said in the *Tikkunei HaZohar* (Corrections of the Zohar, Correction 30, second path), which says[4]: **Rise and awaken for the sake of the *Shechinah* (Divine Presence), for your heart lacks understanding to know about Her [the *Shechinah*], that She is there in your midst.** Get up and awaken yourselves for the sake of the Holy *Shechinah* because you have an empty heart without understanding, to know and perceive Her, even though She is in your midst.

The secret meaning of this is, "A voice says, call" (Isaiah 40:6) as in "Call now, is there any that will answer you? And to which of the holy ones will you turn to?" (Job 5:1) And She [the *Shechinah*] says, "What should I call for? All flesh is dry straw" (Isaiah 40:6), that is, they are all as beasts that eat straw. "And all his kindness is as the flower of the field." (Ibid) Each act of kindness they perform they do it for themselves alone [to receive a benefit]. And even those who engage with the Torah, all the kindness they perform, they do it for themselves alone."

And the secret of the passage: **"A voice says, Call!"** (Isaiah 40:6) is that a voice beats inside the heart of each and every Israelite to call out and pray for the elevation of the Holy *Shechinah* (Divine Presence), who is the collective souls of all the Israelites (and there is evidence from the passage, **"Call now; is there anyone who will answer you?"** (Job 5:1) that "calling" refers to prayer.)

But the *Shechinah* (Divine Presence) says, **"What should I call for?"** (Isaiah 40:6) In other words, I have no power to lift myself up from the dust because **"all flesh is dry straw"** (Ibid), everyone is like beasts eating grass and straw, that is, they do their Precepts

---

מי הם האנשים הגורמים לכל מקרי החורבן וההרס בעולם?

ע) וזה שאמרו בתיקונים (תיקון ל' נתיב תנינא) וז"ל וזה לשונו **קוּמוּ וְאִתְּעָרוּ לְגַבֵּי שְׁכִינְתָּא, דְּאִית לְכוֹן לִבָּא בְּלָא סָכְלְתָנוּ לְמִנְדַּע בָּהּ, וְאִיהוּ בֵּינַיְכוּ.** קומו והתעוררו בשביל השכינה הקדושה, שהרי יש לכן לב ריקן בלי בינה לדעת ולהשיג אותה. אע"פ אף על פי שהיא בתוככם.

וְרָזָא דְמִלָּה "קוֹל אוֹמֵר קְרָא" (ישעיהו מ', ו'), **כְּגוֹן: "קְרָא נָא הֲיֵשׁ עוֹנֶךָ וְאֶל מִי מִקְּדוֹשִׁים תִּפְנֶה" הַשָּׂדֶה (איוב ה', א') וְהִיא אָמְרַת מָה אֶקְרָא, כָּל הַבָּשָׂר חָצִיר, כֹּלָּא אִינוּן כִּבְעִירָן דְּאָכְלִין חָצִיר, וְכָל חַסְדּוֹ כְּצִיץ הַשָּׂדֶה הַשָּׂדֶה** (ישעיהו מ', ו'), **כָּל חֶסֶד דְּעָבְדִּין לְגַרְמַיְיהוּ עָבְדִּין, וַאֲפִילוּ כָּל אִינוּן דְּמִשְׁתַּדְּלִין בְּאוֹרַיְתָא, כָּל חֶסֶד דְּעָבְדִּין לְגַרְמַיְיהוּ עָבְדִּין.**

וסוד הדבר, כמ"ש כמו שכתוב (ישעיה מ') **קוֹל אוֹמֵר קְרָא**, שקול דופק בלבו של כל אחד ואחד מישראל לקרות ולהתפלל להרמת השכינה הקדושה, שהיא כללות נשמות של כל ישראל (ומביא ראיה מהכתוב קרא נא היש עונך, שקריאה פירושו תפילה).

אבל השכינה אומרת **מָה אֶקְרָא**, כלומר אין בי כח להרים את עצמי מעפר, בשביל ש**כָּל הַבָּשָׂר חָצִיר**, כולם המה כבהמות אוכלי עשב וחציר, כלומר שעושים המצות בלי דעת כמו בהמות, **וְכָל חַסְדּוֹ כְּצִיץ הַשָּׂדֶה** (ישעיהו מ', ו'), כל החסדים שעושים, לעצמם הם עושים,

173

without any understanding, just like beasts, **"And all his kindness is as the flower of the field,"** (Ibid) and every act of kindness that they do – is for their themselves alone, meaning that all the Precepts that they fulfill is done without any intention of giving pleasure to the Creator, rather they do the precepts only to benefit themselves.

"And even those who engage with the Torah, all the kindness they perform, they do it for themselves only", [and] even the best of them, who have dedicated their time in engaging with the Torah, did so only to benefit their own self without the proper intention of giving pleasure to their Maker.

At that time, [it is written] about this generation: "A *Ruach* (Spirit) goes by and never returns to the world." (Psalms 78:39) and this is the Spirit of the Messiah, who has to redeem the Israelites from all their troubles until they reach complete redemption in order to fulfill the scriptural passage: "For the earth shall be full of the knowledge of the Creator," etc. (Isaiah 11:9) That Spirit has disappeared and gone away, and does not shine in the world.

Woe to those people who cause [the Spirit] to disappear and go away from the world, never to return, because they make the Torah dry, and they don't want to engage in the wisdom of Kabbalah. Woe to those people who cause that the Spirit of the Messiah to disappear and go away from the world, and never be able to return. They are the ones who make the Torah dry because they do not want to engage with the study of the Wisdom of Kabbalah. That is, without anything "moist" of Wisdom and knowledge.

This is because they restrict themselves only to the practicing part of the Torah. And they do not want to make an effort and understand the Wisdom of Kabbalah, to know and to gain Wisdom in the Secrets of the Torah as well as the reasons of the Precept. **Woe to them that [through these actions] of theirs, they cause poverty and wars and robbery and pillaging and killing and destruction in the world.** End of quote.

כלומר שאין כונתם במצות שעושים, שתהיינה בכדי להשפיע נחת
רוח ליוצרם אלא רק לתועלת עצמם הם עושים המצות.

**וַאֲפִילוּ כָּל אִינּוּן דְּמִשְׁתַּדְּלִין בְּאוֹרַיְתָא, כָּל חֶסֶד דְּעַבְדִין לְגַרְמַיְיהוּ
עַבְדִין.** ואפילו הטובים שבהם, שמסרו זמנם על עסק התורה, לא
עשו זה, אלא לתועלת גופם עצמם. בלי כונה הרצויה, בכדי להשפיע
נ״ר נחת רוח ליוצרם.

בְּהַהוּא זִמְנָא וְכוּ' רוּחַ הוֹלֵךְ וְלֹא יָשׁוּב לְעָלְמָא (תהילים עח', לט'), **וְדָא
אִיהוּ רוּחָא דִּמְשִׁיחַ,** בעת ההיא, רוח הולך ולא ישוב, להעולם,
דהיינו רוח המשיח. הצריך לגאול את ישראל מכל צרותיהם עד לגאולה
השלמה לקיים הכתוב, ומלאה הארץ דעה את ה' וגו' (ישעיהו יא', ט')
הרוח הזה נסתלק לו והלך, ואינו מאיר בעולם.

**וַי לוֹן מָאן דְּגָרְמִין דְּיֵיזִיל לֵיהּ מִן עָלְמָא וְלָא יְתוּב לְעָלְמָא. דְּאִלֵּין
אִינּוּן דְּעַבְדִין לְאוֹרַיְתָא יַבָּשָׁה, וְלָא בָּעָאן לְאִשְׁתַּדְּלָא בְּחָכְמָה
דְקַבָּלָה.** אוי להם לאותם אנשים הגורמים, שרוחו של משיח יסתלק
וילך לו מהעולם, ולא יוכל לשוב לעולם, שהמה, הם העושים את
התורה ליבשה ולא רוצים לעסוק בלמוד חכמת הקבלה, כלומר,
בלי משהו לחלוחית של שכל ודעת.

כי מצטמצמים רק בחלק המעשי של התורה. ואינם רוצים להשתדל
ולהבין בחכמת הקבלה, לידע ולהשכיל בסודות התורה וטעמי
מצוה. **וַי לוֹן דְּגָרְמִין עֲנִיּוּתָא וְחַרְבָּא וּבִיזָה וְהֶרֶג וְאַבְדָן בְּעָלְמָא.** אוי
להם, שהם גורמים במעשיהם הללו, שיהיו עניות ענניות וחרב וחמס וביזה והריגות והשמדות בעולם.
עכ״ל עד כאן לשונו.

71) And the meaning of their words, as we have explained, is that there are those [people] who engage with the Torah and yet despise their own interiority and the interiority of the Torah, putting it aside as something that is not needed in the world and engaging with it only at times that are "neither day nor night," and [as a result] they are with it like blind [people] who are searching a wall. By doing so, they increase their own exteriority, that is, [enhance] their bodily benefit. They also consider the exteriority of the Torah more than they consider the interiority of the Torah. Through these actions, they bring about the increase and strengthening of all the exterior aspects in the world over the interior aspects in the world, every [aspect] according to its own essence, because the exterior of the collective of the Israelites, that is, the ignoramuses among them who are not educated, is strengthened and cancels out the interiority of the collective of Israelites who are the great [sages] of the Torah.

And also the exteriority of the Nations of the World - which [refers to] those among them who spread destruction, become stronger and cancels out their interiority - which are the Righteous from the Nations. And also the exteriority of the entire world, which is the Nations of the World, becomes stronger and cancels out the Israelites, who are the interiority of the world.

And in such a generation, all those who spread destruction among the Nations of the World raise their head and mainly want to wipe out and kill the Israelites. This is as our sages said (Tractate *Yebamot* page 63): "Devastation comes into the world only on the account of the Israelites." That means, as was said in the above *Tikkunim* (in the *Zohar*), that they cause poverty and wars and robberies and killings and destruction in the entire world.

Are you ready to take responsibility?

And indeed we have, due to our many sins, [actually] witnessed all that was said in those *Tikkunim* (in the *Zohar*), and on top of that, the attribute of harsh judgment has struck the best of us. As

עא) וטעם דבריהם הוא, כמו שבארנו, שבהיות כל עוסקי התורה, מזלזלים בפנימיות שלהם, ובפנימיות התורה, ומניחים אותה, כמו דבר שאין צורך בו בעולם, ויעסקו בה רק בשעה שלא יום ולא לילה, והמה בה, כעורים מגששים קיר. שבזה, המה מגבירים את חיצוניותם עצמם, דהיינו תועלת גופם, וכן חיצוניות התורה, המה מחשיבים על פנימיות התורה, ואז המה גורמים במעשיהם הללו, שכל בחינות החיצוניות שישנן בעולם מגבירות את עצמן על כל חלקי הפנימיות שבעולם, כל אחת לפי מהותה, כי החיצוניות שבכלל ישראל, דהיינו עמי הארצות שבהם, מתגברת ומבטלת את הפנימיות שבכלל ישראל שהם גדולי התורה.

וכן החיצוניות שבאומות העולם, שהם בעלי החורבן שבהם, מתגברת ומבטלת את הפנימיות שבהם, שהם חסידי אומות העולם. וכן חיצוניות כל העולם, שהם אוה"ע אומות העולם, מתגברת ומבטלת את בני ישראל, שהם פנימיות העולם.

ובדור כזה, כל בעלי החורבן שבאומות העולם, מרימים ראש, ורוצים בעיקר להשמיד ולהרג את בני ישראל, דהיינו כמ"ש כמו שאמרו ז"ל (יבמות ס"ג) אין פורענות באה לעולם אלא בשביל ישראל. דהיינו כמ"ש כמו שאמרו בתיקונים הנ"ל שהם גורמים עניות וחרב ושוד והריגות והשמדות בעולם כולו.

מהי האחריות המוטלת על הדורות שלנו?

ואחר שבעונותינו הרבים נעשינו עדי ראיה לכל האמור בתיקונים הנ"ל. ולא עוד אלא שמדת הדין פגעה דוקא בהטובים שבנו. כמ"ש

was said (Tractate *Bava Kama* page 60): "Calamity… always begins with the righteous first." And out of all the glory that the Israelites had in the countries of Poland and Lithuania etc, all that remains are the remnants who are in our Holy Land.

So from now on, it is incumbent upon us, the survivors of the destruction, to correct this severe distortion. And each and every one of us, the remnants, should take upon himself, with his whole heart and his whole being, to enhance from here onwards the interiority of the Torah and to give it its rightful place as more important than the exterior part of the Torah. Then each and every one of us will merit the enhancement of the quality of his own interiority, that is, the quality of Israelite in him, which refers to the needs of the soul more than the needs of his external self, which is the aspect of the Nations of the World in him, which alludes to the bodily needs.

And this power will reach the entirety of the Israelites to the point where even the unlearned and uneducated among us will recognize and know the superiority and excellence of the great [sages] of the Israelites and will listen to them and follow them. And the interiority of the Nations of the World, which are the Righteous from the Nations of the World, will become stronger and will vanquish the exteriority, which are the propagators of destruction

And in this way, the interiority of the world, which is the Israelites, will increase in all their superiority and excellence over the exteriority of the world, which are the Nations. And then all the Nations of the World will recognize and admit the advantage that the Israelites have over them. And they will fulfill the scriptural passage: "And the peoples will take them and bring them to their place, and they will settle the Israelites upon the land of the Creator," etc. (Isaiah 14:2). Also: "And they shall bring your sons in their bosom, and your daughters shall be carried on their shoulders." (Isaiah 49:22) And this is what is meant by the passage in the *Zohar*, *Naso* (verse 90) page 124b, that says: **And with this book of yours, which is the Book of the *Zohar*, etc., they shall be go out from exile with mercy,** as explained. Amen, may it be so.

כמו שאמרו ז"ל (ב"ק ס' [מסכת] בבא קמא, עמוד ס') [פורענות] אינה מתחלת אלא מן הצדיקים תחילה. ומכל הפאר שהיה לכלל ישראל בארצות פולין וליטא, וכו', לא נשאר לנו אלא השרידים שבארצנו הקדושה.

הנה מעתה מוטל רק עלינו שארית הפליטה, לתקן את המעוות החמור הזה, וכל אחד ואחד מאתנו שרידי הפליטה, יקבל על עצמו בכל נפשו ומאודו, להגביר מכאן ואילך את פנימיות התורה וליתן לה את מקומה הראוי, כחשיבותה על מעלת חיצוניות התורה, ואז יזכה כל אחד ואחד מאתנו להגביר מעלת פנימיותו עצמו, דהיינו בחינת ישראל שבו, שהיא צרכי הנפש על בחינת חיצוניותו עצמו, שהיא בחינת אוה"ע אומות העולם שבו, שהיא צרכי הגוף.

ויגיע כח הזה גם על כלל ישראל כולו עד שעמי הארצות שבנו, יכירו וידעו את השבח והמעלה של גדולי ישראל עליהם, וישמעו להם ויצייתו להם. וכן פנימיות אוה"ע אומות העולם, שהם חסידי אומות העולם, יתגברו ויכניעו את החיצוניות שלהם. שהם בעלי החורבן.

וכן פנימיות העולם, שהם ישראל יתגברו בכל שבחם ומעלתם על חיצוניות העולם, שהם האומות. ואז כל אוה"ע אומות העולם יכירו וידו במעלת ישראל עליהם. ויקיימו הכתוב (ישעיה י"ד) ולקחום עמים והביאום אל מקומם, והתנחלום בית ישראל על אדמת ה' וגו'. וכן (ישעיה מ"ט) והביאו בניך בחוצן ובנותיך על כתף תנשאנה. וז"ש וזה שכתוב בזוהר נשא (הסולם, סעיף צ') דף קכד ע"ב וז"ל **בהאי חיבורא דילך דאיהו ספר הזהר וכו' יפקון ביה מן גלותא ברחמי** בחיבור הזה שלך, שהוא ספר הזוהר וכו' יצאו בו מן הגלות ברחמים דהיינו כמבואר. אכי"ר אמן כן יהי רצון.

CHART A

The qualities of the Inanimate, Vegetative, Animal and Speaking (Human)

Inanimate	Small Desire to Receive. There is motion inside the Inanimate but it does not develop nor change. There is a collective force of motion and all the parts of the Inanimate act as one. The desire of all type of Inanimate is one: to be. To exist. To neither change nor transform. They all act as collective and not as individuals.
Vegetative	A bigger Desire to Receive. Each type of the Vegetative has a typical desire and each type react differently to changes in the environment. Each type develops differently yet the Desire to Receive is not big enough to push them to interact or move to another location.
Animal	Much bigger Desire to Receive. Each type has a different way of living (some walk, some swim, some crawl and some fly). Their desire enables them to move and change location but is not big enough to have any feeling for each other; they cannot feel the sorrow or the happiness of their fellow friend.
Speaking (Human)	Complete and total degree of the Desire to Receive. Enables to feel all the previous levels of desire and in addition to feel the desire, pain or happiness of others. The difference between the Animal type of desire to the Speaking type is like the difference between one individual created being and the entire existence.

טבלה א'

תכונות הדצח"מ: דומם, צומח, חי ומדבר

דצח"מ	מאפיינים
דומם	רצון לקבל קטן ביותר. קיימת תנועה כוללת בתוך הדומם אבל הוא עצמו לא מתפתח. כל חלקי הדומם פועלים כאחד. הרצון של כל סוגי הדומם הוא אחד: להיות. להתקיים. לא להשתנות. לכן סוגי הדומם פועלים ככלל אחד ולא כפרטים.
צומח	רצון לקבל גדול יותר. כל סוג בצומח רוצה לקבל לעצמו בצורתו האופיינית ולהגיב לשינויים בסביבה לפי תכונותיו. כל פרט מתפתח בצורה שונה אבל הרצון לקבל לא מספיק גדול כדי להניע אותם לפעולת גומלין ביניהם או לזוז ממקומם.
חי	רצון לקבל עוד יותר גדול. לכל סוג בעולם החי יש צורת חיים שונה (אריה שונה מנשר שונה מנחש) ורצון מספיק גדול שמאפשר להם לזוז ממקום למקום. הרצון לקבל לא מספיק כדי להרגיש את הזולת. אין הרגש צער או שמחה של הזולת.
מדבר	רצון לקבל שלם שלם ואינסופי. מאפשר להרגיש את כל חלקי הרצון הקודמים ובנוסף להרגיש את הרצון, הכאב והשמחה של הזולת. רצון זה גדול מן הרצון הקודם לו (עולם החי) כמו המרחק בין פרט אחד בבריאה מול כל המציאות כולה.

CHART B
Four levels of development of the Desire

First Division	In this phase we expand our Ego without boundaries and attain the biggest physical Desire to Receive. The more our ego and desire are flawed, meaning bigger and stronger, the more we can correct. Therefore our physical Desire must grow under the dominion of and be subjected to the ego and the system of the *Klippot* (Negative Shells). Our Desire is nourished by the *Klippot* (and not by the Light) therefore our fulfillment is temporary and the Desire is then doubled. It is then nourished by the *Klippot* (and not by the Light) and the fulfillment is again temporary and the Desire is then again doubled. This goes on like a vicious circle for the first 13 (for boys) or 12 (for girls) years of our life.
Second Division	From age of *Bar/Bat Mitzvah* the point in the heart is being awakened and work under the dominion of the Worlds of Holiness. The main purpose of the point is to achieve and enlarge the ***spiritual*** Desire to Receive. The excessive Desire to Receive is completed only when it is a Desire to Receive spirituality. This phase is considered as the "maidservant who is serving her mistress", because it transforms the Desire to Receive (Not For Its Own Sake) into Desire to Receive for the Sake of Sharing (For Its Own Sake). The purpose of this phase is to bring the person to fall in love with the Creator with great passion, similar to an inflamed passion of material lust. This will awaken the five parts of the Soul.

<u>טבלה ב'</u>
ארבעת שלבי התפתחות הרצון

שלב שבו מגדילים את האגו הגשמי ללא גבול ומשיגים את הרצון לקבל הגשמי הגדול ביותר. ככל שהרצון והאגו מקולקלים יותר, כלומר גדולים יותר - יש יותר מה לתקן. לכן צריך שהרצון הגשמי יגדל תחת שליטת האגו והקליפות הגשמיות. הקליפות (לא האור) מזינות את הרצון ולכן לא רק שהסיפוק הוא זמני אלא הרצון מוכפל ושוב הרצון מוגשם על ידי הקליפות והספוק הוא זמני והרצון מוכפל שנית וחוזר חלילה. תהליך זה נמשך במשך 12 (לבנות) או 13 (לבנים) השנים הראשונות של חיינו.	חלוקה א'
מגיל בר/בת מצווה הנקודה שבלב מתחילה להתעורר ולתפקד תחת מערכת הקדושה. תפקיד הנקודה: להגדיל את הרצון לקבל ***הרוחני***. רצון מושלם הוא צרוף של רצון גשמי ורצון רוחני ביחד. רצון לקבל רוחני גורם לאדם לרצות מלוי גם לנשמה. שלב זה נחשב לשפחה כי הוא יכול לשרת את הרצון לקבל ("לא לשמה") ולהפוך אותו לרצון לקבל על מנת לתת ("לשמה"). המטרה של שלב זה היא להביא את האדם להתאהב בבורא בתאווה גדולה כמו תאווה גשמית ולעורר את חמשת חלקי הנשמה.	חלוקה ב'

Third Division	A phase of spiritual work For Its Own Sake without any personal agenda. We purify the Desire to Receive for the Self Alone and turn it into a Desire to Share. Then we can receive the five parts of the Soul, which are called *Nefesh* (Lower Soul), *Ruach* (Spirit), *Neshamah* (Soul), *Chayah* (Life-Sustaining), and *Yechidah* from their source in the Endless World.
Fourth Division	The spiritual work after the Resurrection of the Dead. The Desire to Receive has been completely absent through death and burial of many past life times. In this phase the Desire to Receive (known as "defect" or "flaw") returns and is again alive with the greatest form of excessive Desire to Receive but works now ***only*** for the sake of sharing.

חלוקה ג'	שלב של עבודה רוחנית לשמה, ללא אג'נדה אישית. בשלב זה מטהרים את הרצון לקבל שיהיה רק על מנת לתת. ואז יוכל לקבל את חמשת חלקי הנשמה (נפש, רוח, נשמה, חיה, יחידה) ממקורן באינסוף.
חלוקה ד'	העבודה הרוחנית אחרי תחיית המתים. בשלבים הקודמים נעלם הרצון לקבל לגמרי על ידי תהליכי המיתה והקבורה במחזורי החיים השונים. בשלב הנוכחי הרצון לקבל (הנקרא "מום") קם לתחייה בעוצמה כמו חלוקה א' וחלוקה ב', אבל עובד *רק* על מנת לתת.

Glossary

13 Years – When a boy reaches 13 years of age, he goes through the process of Bar Mitzvah, where he receives an additional part of the soul called *Ruach* and assumes responsibility for his spiritual actions, which until now belonged to his parents. See also: Spirit

70 Nations of the World – All the souls that come down to our world are divided into 70 nations, which are 70 levels of souls. The Israelites are in a separate category. See also: Israelite

248 – There are 248 bone segments in the human body as well as 248 words in the *Shema* prayer and 248 positive Precepts. These positive Precepts are the proactive "do" actions, and each one relates to a different part of the body. When we perform these Precepts, we are strengthening our body. See also: 365, 613

365 – There are 365 tendons and sinews in the human body as well as 365 negative Precepts. These negative Precepts are the proactive "do not do" actions, referring to acts of restriction and refraining from acting on our negative and selfish impulses. Each Precept corresponds to a different sinew and tendon, and to each of the 365 days of the year. See also: 248, 613

613 – The number of Precepts—spiritual actions—that we can do to get spiritually closer to the Light of the Creator. There are 613 Precepts, and all can be found within the *Five Books of Moses*. These Precepts are divided into two categories: 248 Precepts of proactive/positive "do" actions, and 365 Precepts of proactive/negative "do not do" actions. Performing both types of Precepts will bring us closer to the Creator. See also: Precept, 248, 365

2000 Years of Chaos – The first era of the world is called the 2000 Years of Chaos because it was during this time that everything was still falling into place (the Creation of the World, Noah's Flood, Tower of Babel, etc). The *Talmud* and Rashi tell us that these 2000 years ended when Abraham was 52 years old, and that all civilizations that had existed prior to this point had lived in a chaotic state of mind, enslaved by their Desire to Receive for the Self Alone. See also: 6000 Years of *Tikkun*

2000 Years of Messiah – The third and last era of the world, starting from the time the *Mishnah* was written down; this era will end with the coming of Messiah. See also: 6000 Years of *Tikkun*

2000 Years of Torah – The second era of the world, starting 48 years prior to the birth of Isaac in the third millennium BCE and carrying through to the Giving of the Torah on Mount Sinai and the building of both Holy Temples in Jerusalem. In this era, the Torah, *Mishnah*, and *Talmud* flourished, hence the name "2000 Years of Torah." See also: 6000 Years of *Tikkun*

6000 Years of *Tikkun* – *Tikkun* means "correction," and these 6000 years begin with the Creation of the World and extend to the end of the sixth millennium after Creation. The correction we must do is correcting the sin of Adam and Eve, who ate from the Tree of Knowledge, which is a code for them having listened to and acted on their selfish desires. The 6000 Years of *Tikkun* are divided into three eras, each consisting of 2000 years. See also: 2000 Years of Chaos, 2000 Years of Messiah, 2000 Years of Torah

Abayey – A kabbalist sage from the time of the *Talmud* (300–400 CE).

Adam Kadmon – See: Primordial Man

Angels – Frequencies or packets of spiritual intelligent-energy beings that constantly roam and move about among us, acting as messengers from the Creator and affecting things that happen in our daily life. We can imagine an angel as being a conduit or channel that transports cosmic energy or thoughts from one place to another or from one spiritual dimension to another. Angels have no free will, and each angel is dedicated to one specific purpose.

Animal Kingdom – The third of the Four Kingdoms (Inanimate, Vegetative, Animal, and Speaking). This kingdom has a larger capacity of the Desire to Receive than both the Inanimate and

Vegetative Kingdoms, but a lesser capacity than the Speaking Kingdom. See also: Inanimate Kingdom, Speaking Kingdom, Vegetative Kingdom

Ari – Rav Isaac Luria, often called "the Ari" or "Holy Lion," was born in 1534 in Jerusalem and died in 1572 in the city of Safed in the Galilee region of Israel. Considered to be the father of contemporary Kabbalah, the Ari was a foremost kabbalistic scholar and the founder of the Lurianic method of learning and teaching Kabbalah. His closest student, Rav Chaim Vital, compiled and wrote the Ari's teachings word-for-word in 18 volumes. These 18 volumes are collectively known as the *Writings of the Ari*. See also: *Tree of Life*

Asiyah – See: World of Action

Attributes (*Midot*) – Literally "measurements" or "levels," *Midot* refers to the quantity of Light that is revealed through the *Sefirot*. Exodus 34:6-7 lists the Thirteen Attributes that describe the different aspects of the Creator. See also: Ten *Sefirot*

Atzilut – See: World of Emanation

Back – The term used to describe those times when it feels as if the Creator has turned His "Back" on us. When we understand the system of cause and effect but we do not immediately see the good behind an apparently negative situation, we have two choices: to succumb to our doubt and say that the Creator has deserted us, or to choose to understand that everything that happens is part of a bigger picture and that we cannot see right now the ultimate good that will come. The sages explain that the Period of the Back, although painful to the person experiencing it, always comes right before a Period of the Face, which represents complete fulfillment

Beauty – See: *Tiferet*

Bestow Goodness – The Creator is a completely sharing Being. All He wants is to share with us and to give us endless fulfillment, pleasure, and joy. This was the original Thought of Creation: To create a "Vessel" that would be able to receive all the pleasure that the Creator wanted to give because the nature of the Good is to bestow goodness. See also: Thought of Creation

Between a Person and His Friend – This is a term used when describing Precepts of the Torah that have to do with the relationship between a person and his fellow man, like "Honor your father and mother," "Do not kill," "Do not steal," "Return a lost object," etc. See also: 248, 365, 613, Precept

Between a Person and the Creator – This is a term used when describing Precepts of the Torah that have to do with the relationship between a person and the Creator, like connecting to the energy of Holidays, meditations, etc. See also: 248, 365, 613, Precept

Beriah – See: World of Creation.

Binah (**Understanding**) – The third of the Ten *Sefirot* (levels). *Binah* is the direct channel that funnels the Light of the Creator through the other levels and into our physical world. *Binah* serves as a store and source of energy—physical, emotional, intellectual, and spiritual—for our whole universe. It stands for the universal "mother figure." See also: Head, *Sefirot*, Upper Three, World, World of Creation.

Book of Formation (*Sefer Yetzirah*) – The earliest known book of kabbalistic knowledge and wisdom. Written by Abraham the Patriarch some 3800 years ago, it deals primarily with the intrinsic power within the Aramaic-Hebrew letters and the stars, and how both the letters and the stars affect us in this world. All the secrets of Creation that will eventually be revealed are considered to be concealed in this book.

Chamber – The spiritual space in which we receive all the good that exists for eternity.

Chasadim (Mercies), **Light of** – When a person awakens in himself a desire for the Light of the Creator through transforming his Desire to Receive for the Sake of Sharing, he creates a new Light that is called the Light of *Chasadim*. This Light clothes the Light of *Chochmah*, which is the essence of the Light of the Creator, and thus enables the Vessel to contain and hold It. See also: *Chochmah*, Clothing

Chaya (Life-Sustaining) – The fourth part of a person's soul, called *Chaya*, is very rarely received because it denotes that the person has achieved such a high level of spirituality that he no longer has the Evil Inclination within him. *Chaya* is the Light of the *Sefira* of *Chochmah*, which provides life and sustains it. See also: *Chochmah*, *Nefesh, Neshama, Ruach, Yechida*

Chesed (Mercy) – The fourth of the Ten *Sefirot* (levels). *Chesed* is the absolute representation of the Right Column energy, the positive pole of the spiritual energy which is sharing. *Chesed* holds the still-undifferentiated seeds of Creation. The Chariot (*Merkavah*) for the *Sefira* of *Chesed* is Abraham the Patriarch. See also: Chest, *Sefirot*

Chest – Of the Ten *Sefirot*, the six lower ones—*Chesed, Gevurah, Tiferet, Netzach, Hod,* and *Yesod*—were compressed into one, called *Zeir Anpin*. The top three (*Chesed, Gevurah,* and *Tiferet*) are called the "Chest" of *Zeir Anpin*. See also: *Sefirot, Chesed, Gevurah, Tiferet, Netzach, Hod, Yesod*

Chest Downwards – This term refers to the bottom three *Sefirot* of *Zeir Anpin*: *Netzach, Hod,* and *Yesod.* See also: *Sefirot, Netzach, Hod, Yesod*

Chochmah (Wisdom) – The second of the Ten *Sefirot* (levels). A level of energy where the end result of the most complicated process is known at the very beginning. *Chochmah* contains the totality of the Light and stands for the universal "father figure." See also: *Sefirot*, World

Cleaving – A concept describing how close we should be to the Creator. We need to cleave and be as one with the Creator. In spirituality, closeness is determined not by space or distance, but by Similarity of Form. The closer we are to behaving like the Creator, the closer we get to becoming like God. When we act selfishly, reactively, or negatively, we distance ourselves from the Creator and are not cleaving to Him, but when we act selflessly—like the Creator—we become closer to Him.

Clothing – All spiritual energy like the Lightforce of the Creator needs to be concealed to be revealed; this concealment is referred to as "clothing." Our thoughts, words, and actions are clothing for the Lightforce of the Creator. Our body is the clothing for our soul. The Torah is the clothing for the Creator. When a *Partzuf* receives assistance from a lower *Partzuf*, then the lower one is a garment or clothing to the upper *Partzuf*. See also: *Partzuf*

Concealed Torah – The aspects of the Torah whose meaning is hidden; also called the Secrets of the Torah. The Concealed Torah is essentially a reference to the Wisdom of Kabbalah. One reason that Kabbalah is referred to as the Concealed Torah is because it is concealed from the immediate and literal understanding of the Torah. Another reason is that the Creator is concealing Himself in the Torah. See also: *Sitrei Torah*

Correction – See: *Tikkun*

Coarse/Thick – A term describing the level of our Desire to Receive.

Creator – The Endless Light or the Lightforce of the God; the Cause of all causes.

Crown – See: *Keter*

Days of Messiah – The 1000 years of pure happiness, pleasure, bliss, joy, and fulfillment. In the Days of Messiah, there will be no death, no intolerance, no hatred. See also: 2000 Years of Messiah

Death Is Eternally Swallowed – During the Days of Messiah, there will be no more death. It will be swallowed up forever by the Light of the Creator. This term also refers to the Resurrection of the Dead that will happen when Messiah comes. See also: 2000 Years of Messiah

Desire – A measurement of how much we are willing to work for and earn that which we want to have or achieve. There can be no action at all of any kind without some form of desire, whether conscious or subconscious.

Deuteronomy, Book of – The fifth book of the *Five Books of Moses*, also known as *Devarim* (lit. words). Deuteronomy details the review given to the children of Israel by Moses of the 40 years they had spent in the desert. This entire book takes place in the time span of one month, ending with Moses' death and the children of Israel's entry into the land of Israel.

Difference of Form – The opposite form to that of the Creator; that is, acting through selfish impulses instead of sharing selflessly. The Creator is a completely sharing Being. That is His Form. When we act selfishly and do not share selflessly, we are in Difference of Form with the Creator. We are not cleaving to Him, but instead distancing ourselves. This is the opposite of Similarity of Form. See also: Cleaving, Similarity of Form

Ephraim – The second of two sons born to Joseph the Righteous. Ephraim and his brother, Menashe, headed of the 12 Tribes in the desert with Moses.

Ein Sof (Endless) – Before the creation of this world, the endless Light of the Creator filled all existence. There was no lack of any kind. All desires were completely fulfilled, and the Vessel, which is the Desire to Receive, was not blemished by the Desire to Receive for the Self Alone.

End of the *Tikkun* – When we collectively have transformed our nature so that we become completely sharing beings, when we are in true Similarity of Form with the Creator, we will have reached the End of the *Tikkun* (lit. fixing/correction), and the Days of Messiah will arrive. See also: Days of Messiah, Similarity of Form

Essence of the Creator – This can be described as a Being of pure, unconditional sharing. However, limited as we are by our five senses, we cannot truly understand what the Creator's essence is, just as we cannot truly comprehend how long infinity can be. Such concepts are simply beyond our mental abilities.

Eternity/Victory – See: *Netzach*

***Etz HaChayim* (*Tree of Life*)** – The first four volumes in the 18-volume set of the *Writings of the Ari*, written by Rav Isaac Luria (the Ari) and compiled by his student, Rav Chaim Vital. These volumes contain the main teachings of the *Study of the Ten Luminous Emanations*. See also: Ari, *Ten Luminous Emanations*

Exile – The state of existence where we are less connected and less in tune with the Light, a state where chaos rules and miracles are rare. This state was brought about by the destruction of both Holy Temples. The Hebrew word for "exile" is *Galut*, which also means "to reveal" because this state of existence will change permanently once we reveal the Wisdom of Kabbalah, spread it to everyone, and thus change the world.

Exterior Aspect – All spiritual energy like the Lightforce of the Creator needs to be concealed to be revealed. The exterior aspect through which the Lightforce is revealed is referred to as "clothing." See also: Clothing

First Generations – The people who lived at the beginning of the *Tikkun* process are called the First Generations. They were very high and powerful souls, and therefore the Light they revealed was strong. However, when they were negative, the darkness they could cause was equally powerful and the destruction they brought to the world was chaotic.

For Its Own Sake – Doing something just for the sake of revealing the Light, without any personal agenda or ulterior thought behind it. This term is commonly said about the study of the Torah and the Precepts. In Hebrew, it is called *Lishma* (lit. For Its Own Sake). See also: Not For Its Own Sake, Precept

Foundation – See: *Yesod*

Fourth Phase – There are four phases in the development of the Desire to Receive, from the purest to the densest. The fourth phase of the Desire to Receive is when the individual completes the desire to be the purest Vessel for the Light of the Creator. See also: Vessel

Free Will – This is a concept that we find in all religions and philosophies. The concept is that we came here with free will as opposed to our life being preordained. The kabbalists say that we have free will so that we can transform our Desire to Receive for the Self Alone to the Desire to Receive for the Sake of Sharing.

Garden of Eden – See: Paradise

Gevurah (Judgment/Might) – The fifth of the Ten *Sefirot* (levels). *Gevurah* is the direct representation of Left Column energy. The Chariot for the *Sefira* of *Gevurah* is Isaac the Patriarch. See also: Chest, *Sefirot*

Giving Pleasure to the Maker – When we engage our life in the Torah and the Precepts, and transform our Desire to Receive for the Self Alone to the Desire to Share, we create an affinity with the Creator, our Maker, and this affinity gives pleasure (so to speak) to our Maker.

Glory – See: *Hod*

Haman – An evil descendant of the tribe of Amalek (from the Bible), who tried to completely wipe out the Jews with the help of the Persian king Ahasuerus (aka Xerxes I), but Queen Esther and her uncle, Mordechai, foiled his plans and saved the Jews. The whole story is found in the Scroll of Esther. This event took place few years before the Jews returned from their 70 years of exile.

HaSulam – Literally "the Ladder," this is a commentary on the *Zohar* written by Rav Ashlag. Rav Ashlag translated the entire *Zohar* from Aramaic to Hebrew, including with the translation his commentary, which he called *HaSulam*, a ladder or stepping stone to understanding the hidden secrets coded within the *Zohar*.

He Who Knows All Mysteries – The Lightforce of the Creator.

Head, Middle, and End – The first 2000 years of the *Tikkun* are referred to as the Head and comprise the *Sefirot* of *Chochmah* (Wisdom), *Binah* (Understanding), and *Da'at* (Knowledge); the second 2000 years of the *Tikkun* are referred to as the Middle and comprise the *Sefirot* of *Chesed* (Mercy), *Gevurah* (Judgment), and *Tiferet* (Splendor); the last 2000 years of the *Tikkun* are referred to as the End and comprise the *Sefirot* of *Netzach* (Eternity), *Hod* (Glory), and *Yesod* (Foundation). See also: 6000 Years of *Tikkun*, *Sefirot*

Hell – A purgatory-like place where souls that have moved on but require cleansing from the negativity they revealed while alive go; here all their negativity is purified. The souls remain in Hell no longer than 12 months to complete the purification process.

Hod **(Glory)** – The eighth of the Ten *Sefirot* (levels). *Hod* is an additional connection to the energy of the Left Column, although less intense than *Gevurah*. The Chariot for the *Sefira* of *Hod* is Aaron the High Priest. See also: Chest, Chest Downwards, *Gevurah*, *Sefirot*

Holiness – A term used to describe the level where a person is battling and resisting his ego and the Evil Inclination, and is sharing selflessly instead. This concept is also used to describe items or places and the level of connection we can make through them to the Light. For example, Jerusalem is called the Holy City because it is the energy center of the world and thus, it is where we can make our strongest connection to the Creator.

I Will Hasten It – In the *Book of Isaiah*, 60:22, there is a section that speaks about the days of the Final Redemption, where there is no more war and bloodshed, no more chaos and suffering. If we change our selfish nature and thus earn this merit, then the Creator says to Isaiah, "I will hasten it" – meaning He will bring about the Redemption earlier. See also: In Its Time

Impure System – The Negative Side, the ego, the Evil Inclination, the Satan. The Impure System has only two columns—the Right and Left Columns—without the Central Column to balance the flow of Light and energy. This creates a short circuit in our soul, which fuels the Negative Side, the Satan.

Impurity – A term used to describe the level where a person is failing to resist his ego and the Evil Inclination, and thus is sinking lower and lower into selfishness.

In Its Time – In the *Book of Isaiah*, 60:22, there is a section that speaks about the days of the Final Redemption, where there is no more war and bloodshed, no more chaos and suffering. If we have not changed our selfish nature and we continue in our negative ways of life, then the Creator says to Isaiah that the Redemption will come "in its time" – meaning by the end of the 6000 years of *Tikkun*, and not earlier. See also: 6000 Years of *Tikkun*, I Will Hasten It

Inanimate Kingdom – Of the four Kingdoms (Inanimate, Vegetative, Animal, and Speaking), this is the first and lowest level, representing the lowest intensity of the Desire to Receive. See also: Animal Kingdom, Speaking Kingdom, Vegetative Kingdo

Isaiah – One of the greatest prophets (circa 740 BCE) who preached for social justice based on understanding the Providence of the Creator. As a kabbalistic prophet, Isaiah urged people to reconnect to spirituality rather than to dogmatic religion. He prophesized the End of Days when there would be peace on Earth and a reality where "a wolf shall dwell with a lamb."

Israelite – A code name for anyone who is following a spiritual path and who is working on his or her negative traits and constantly striving to transform them to positive ones. Israelites are people who take upon themselves the responsibility for spreading the Light, putting other people's needs before their own, following the spiritual rules of cause and effect, and not taking the Torah literally but rather as a coded message.

Jeremiah – A prophet that lived in Judah during the time of the First Holy Temple, around 2600 years ago. The book of his prophecies and teachings to the Israelites is called the *Book of Jeremiah*, and it is one of the 24 books of the Bible. He tried to make the Israelites see that worshipping idols was not the right way to connect to the Creator, but he was not listened to and was beaten and imprisoned by the king. He is credited with authoring (through the prophecy of God) the *Book of Lamentations*, another of the 24 Books of the Bible.

Judgment/Might – See: *Gevurah*

Kavanah **(Intention, Meditation)** – The act of centering our consciousness with the attention appropriate to a situation or connection.

Keter **(Crown)** – The first and highest of the Ten *Sefirot* (levels) and the link between the Endless and the Worlds. *Keter* emphasizes the ultimate connection to the Lightorce of the Creator. *Keter* is the seed level and the source of every spiritual and physical dimension. As the seed, it contains all future manifestations. See also: *Sefirot*, World

Kilkul **(Damage), World of** – According to the kabbalists, our physical world manifests everything based on either the World of

Kilkul or the World of *Tikkun* (Correction). Our selfish reactions manifest the World of *Kilkul*, bringing chaos and suffering, while our positive actions manifest the World of *Tikkun*, where we correct the suffering in this world and bring happiness and fulfillment. See also: 6000 Years of *Tikkun, Tikkun*

Kingdom – See: *Malchut*

Klippot – See: Shells

Ladder – See: *HaSulam*

Last Generations – The generations that will bring about the time when world peace will prevail and humanity as a whole will have transformed itself into unique individuals who use their uniqueness to share with others rather than to Receive for the Self Alone. See also: Messiah

Light of the Creator – This Light is the total energy that is received in all the Worlds. It is everything except the Vessel—that is, the Desire to Receive.

Maimonides – See: Rambam

Malchut **(Kingdom)** – The tenth and lowest of the Ten *Sefirot* (levels) in which the greatest Desire to Receive is manifested. *Malchut* represents manifestation, our physical world in which the *Tikkun* process takes place, and every physical connection we make. The Chariot for the *Sefira* of *Malchut* is King David. See also: *Sefirot, Tikkun*

Mercy – See: *Chesed*

Merit – In Hebrew, this word is *zechut*, which is derived from the root word for "pure," meaning that when we transform our selfish nature into one of selflessness and sharing with others, we become pure. In doing so, we will attain the merit of a spiritual lifeline, which will be there when we most need it to remove the chaos, pain, and suffering we are experiencing.

Messiah – Often described as a person, the concept of Messiah simply means the collective consciousness of humanity where everyone cares about others' needs ahead of their own, in this way emulating the complete selflessness of the Light. The concept of death (in health, business, relationships, or anything else) cannot exist within the realm of this consciousness.

Moses – Also known as *Moshe Rabbeinu* (Moses our Teacher), Moses is the greatest prophet to have ever lived. He was able to speak to God almost face-to-face, and he served as the intermediary for the children of Israel to receive the Ten Utterances from God. He took the children of Israel all the way to the Jordan but did not lead them into the land of Israel.

Mount Sinai – The mountain in the Sinai Desert where the children of Israel received the Ten Utterances from God through Moses. Moses spent 40 days and 40 nights on this mountain before bringing down the Two Tablets (the Torah).

Nefesh – The lowest part of our soul, the part that every person is born with. It allows the *Klipot* to connect to us. *Nefesh* is usually fueled by the Desire to Receive for the Self Alone; it is the animal instinct and psyche that we all have. The Torah teaches us that the connection to *Nefesh* is through the blood, and this is why we do not eat or drink anything that has animal blood on it: We do not want to connect to the raw animal instinct of that animal. Throughout a person's life, at certain age-related milestones, he or she receives additional parts of the soul. See also: *Chaya, Klipot, Neshama, Ruach, Yechida*

Neshama (**Soul**) – This is the third part of our soul, which we receive when we reach the age of 20. It is called "Soul" because until we receive this third part, our own soul is not yet complete. This third part of the soul allows us to connect directly to the power of the Creator. It is the Light that is contained in *Binah*. See also: *Binah, Chaya, Nefesh, Ruach, Yechida*

***Netzach* (Eternity/Victory)** – The seventh of the ten levels (*Sefirot*). *Netzach* is an additional connection to the energy of the Right Column, although less powerful than *Chesed*. The Chariot for the *Sefira* of *Netzach* is Moses. See also: *Chesed*, Chest, Chest Downwards, *Sefirot*

Not For Its Own Sake – A concept also known as *Lo Lishma*, this refers to a spiritual action that is done with a hidden agenda, where you are trying to get something for yourself alone. See also: For Its Own Sake

Oneness – See: *Yechida*

Other Side – The Negative Side, the Evil Inclination, the Satan.

Panim Me'irot Umasbirot – A commentary written by the great Kabbalist Rav Ashlag about the *Study of the Ten Luminous Emanations* written by the Ari in the *Etz HaChaim* volumes of the *Writings of the Ari*. See also: Ari, *Tree of Life*

Paradise – The 99% Realm where the Creator is, where there is no chaos, pain or suffering but only happiness and fulfillment. It is conceptually the counter-image of the miseries of human civilization.

Part of God Above – Every single person has a soul, which is a spark of God inside of him or her. This spark is a small part of God, a part of the collective.

Partzuf – A complete spiritual structure of the Ten *Sefirot* that creates a perfect relationship between the Light and the Vessel. A *Partzuf* represents both the Head (the Upper Three *Sefirot*, or potential; and the Body (the Lower Seven *Sefirot*), or actual. See also: Head-Middle-End, Ten *Sefirot*, World

Permission from Heaven – The secrets of Kabbalah are often so revolutionary that if revealed at the wrong time, they would create more chaos than order. Kabbalists throughout the ages have always required Heavenly Permission to reveal such secrets, and only when this permission was given, were they able to teach and reveal these secrets.

Pirkei DeRav Eliezer – A *Midrash* written by Rav Eliezer ben Horkenos in the first century AD about the *Book of Genesis*, part of the *Book of Exodus*, and a few verses in the *Book of Numbers*.

Point – This is a concept used to describe the ultimate and complete Desire to Receive. A point or a dot does not contain anything of its own inside it; therefore, it can contain everything including the infinite Light of the Creator. A circle of any size, on the other hand, is limited by its dimensions to receive only the amount of Light it can hold inside. This shows us that the only true way to receive the ultimate Light of goodness and fulfillment is to be like the point— humble and selfless—because when we expand our ego into a circle, we are limiting the Light that can come to us.

Proverbs, Book of – One of the 24 Books of the Bible. The *Book of Proverbs* was written by King Solomon and deals with life lessons.

Precept – One of the 613 spiritual actions we can do to connect to the Light of the Creator. There are two types of Precepts: those between man and his fellow man, and those between man and the Creator. In Hebrew, the word for Precept is *Mitzvah*, meaning "unity" or "bonding," because the Precepts create unity between the Creator and us. See also: 613, Between a Person and His Friend, Between a Person and the Creator

Primordial Man (*Adam Kadmon*) – The fifth and highest spiritual World. There are four spiritual Worlds that our soul ascends and descends through during the course of the day as we make our spiritual connections. However, there is a fifth World that is even higher than these four—a World that we cannot reach through our connections—and this fifth World is called Primordial Man. See also: World, World of Emanation, World of Creation, World of Formation, World of Action

Prologue of the *Zohar* – The first volume of the *Zohar*. The prologue contains sections of commentary that do not relate specifically to any one portion; it also contains many sections that detail numerous esoteric concepts.

Prophet – A man or woman that was so connected to the Creator that he or she could speak with Him, whether directly, through an additional medium, or in dreams. The prophet served as the connection between the children of Israel and God. Nowadays, the only prophecies that exist appear to us through our dreams, although because of our ego and selfish desires, these dreams often get muddled and their true meaning is lost or misconstrued.

Psalms, Book of – One of the 24 Books of the Bible. The *Book of Psalms* was written by King David and consists of songs and poems that teach us about life and about our personal relationship with the Creator. Many prayers are based on various Psalms, and the *Zohar* often quotes this book.

Pure – Without spiritual blemish. Someone or something that is completely cleansed of negativity. Someone who has less of a Desire to Receive and more of a Desire to Share. The purer a person is, the more Light can shine through him and illuminate his life and the lives of others around him.

Purifies the Body: The essence of the body is the Desire to Receive for the Self Alone, so to purify the body means to reduce that selfish desire and to help transform it to the Desire to Receive for the Sake of Sharing.

Rav Moshe de Leon – A sage and kabbalist living in 13th century Spain. He uncovered and published the *Zohar* manuscripts that had been concealed since being written by Rav Shimon bar Yochai some 1100 years earlier.

Rav Shimon bar Yochai – A great scholar and kabbalist from the time of the *Mishnah* (first century CE). The Talmud tells us that he criticized the Roman Empire and was forced to go into hiding with his son in a cave for 13 years, where he and his son learned all the secrets of the *Zohar* with Elijah the Prophet. After he and his son left the cave, he revealed all these secrets to his other eight students, and they were written down and then buried. Because he authored the *Zohar*, Rav Shimon is considered one of the greatest kabbalists to ever live.

Rambam – An acronym for Rav Moshe ben Maimon, also known as Maimonides. A Rav, scholar, philosopher, and physician who was born in Spain in 1135 and died in Egypt in 1204. The Rambam wrote the *Mishneh Torah* (*Repetition of the Torah*), a compilation of 14 books about every single aspect of *Halachah*. His thoughts strongly influenced all philosophical thinking through his major book *Moreh Nebuchim* (*A Guide for the Perplexed*).

Rav Elazar ben Shimon – Son of the author of the *Zohar*, the great kabbalist Rav Shimon bar Yochai. Around 2000 years ago, Rav Elazar and his father hid in a cave from the Romans for 13 years, and that is where they revealed the Wisdom of the *Zohar*.

Rav Isaac Luria – See: Ari

Rav Pappa - A kabbalist sage from the time of the *Talmud* (300–400 CE).

Receiving for the Sake of Sharing – An action of receiving where the purpose is not to receive *per se*, but to "share" with the giver by accepting what he has to offer and thus making the giver happy. This is not real receiving because ultimately one is not receiving for oneself but for the other person, so this kind of receiving is actually a positive action.

Repentance (*Teshuvah*) – The Hebrew word *teshuvah* means literally "to return." Repentance should be understood as a change of thought and action that we make to correct a wrong we have done. By doing so, we change our consciousness: We take responsibility and own up to our past mistakes, thereby preemptively removing whatever chaos and pain we might face in the future as a result of our negativity. Thus we "return" back to the future.

Resurrection of the Dead – In the Days of Messiah, there will be no more death, and everyone who previously died will come back to life and be with us again. The great Kabbalist Rav Ashlag also explains that during the time of Messiah, everyone will be resurrected with their defects, which is a code word for their selfish natures and characteristics, but these "defects" will be transformed and made pure. See also: Days of Messiah

Returning Light – This is the Supernal Light when it is being rejected and reflected back by the Vessel—that is, by the Desire to Receive—and is thus revealed and manifested.

Revealed Torah – The simple literal meaning of the written Torah, *Mishnah*, and *Talmud*. See also: *Ta'amei Torah*

Root – As creations of God, we can be likened to branches on a tree, whereas God is the root that gives the branches life. Everything (for example, receiving selfishly, reactive behavior) that is bad for the root (God) is bad for the branch (us), and vice versa.

Righteous (*Tzadik*) – A person who is completely devoted to working on transforming his negative traits and to sharing unconditionally with others. The *Midrash* also tells us that this is a person whose positive actions outweigh his negative ones.

Ruach (Spirit) – Of the five levels that make up the soul, *Ruach* is the next level up from the bottom. It is an additional part of our soul that enters us when we reach Bar/Bat Mitzvah (age 13 for a boy, 12 for a girl), and it activates our free will to choose between Light and darkness. See also: *Chaya, Nefesh, Neshama, Yechida*

Sage – A term used to refer to kabbalists living in the time of the Second Temple (516 BCE – 70 CE). These sages were all very wise men who left us with deep wisdom and many lessons to be found in the *Mishnah*, the *Talmud*, and the *Zohar*.

Secrets of the Torah – See: *Sitrei Torah*.

Sefirot – The ten levels of curtains or veils that clothe the raw naked Lightforce of the Creator. The Ten *Sefirot* are (from the top down): *Keter* (Crown), *Chochmah* (Wisdom), *Binah* (Understanding), *Chesed* (Mercy), *Gevurah* (Judgment/Might), *Tiferet* (Beauty), *Netzach* (Eternity/Victory), *Hod* (Glory), *Yesod* (Foundation), and *Malchut* (Kingdom). They are ten Vessels that reveal the Light; the greater the Desire, the higher the level of consciousness that is revealed. The singular of *Sefirot* is *Sefira*. See also: *Keter, Chochmah, Binah, Chesed, Gevurah, Tiferet, Netzach, Hod, Yesod, Malchut*

Shechinah (**Divine Presence**) – The Light of the Creator at its closest frequency to the physical world. The *Shechinah* is the collective soul of all Israelites.

Shells (*Klipot*) – Evil husks created by mankind's negative deeds, the *Klipot* are a metaphysical negative covers that hide the Light of the Creator from us and give it to the Negative or Other Side. They also latch on to the sparks of Light when we fail to act on a positive impulse or action, or when we perform a selfish or negative action. See also: Concealment of the Face, Other Side

Similarity of Form – The Creator is a completely sharing Being. That is His Form. When we act selflessly and do not receive selfishly, we are in Similarity of Form to the Creator. We are cleaving to Him, getting closer to His Supernal splendor. See also: Cleaving, Difference of Form

Sitrei Torah – The concealed wisdom of Kabbalah and the Torah. All secrets and teachings of Kabbalah and the Torah can be divided into two categories: *Sitrei Torah* and *Ta'amei Torah*. *Sitrei Torah* (lit. Secrets of the Torah) refers to the Wisdom of Kabbalah that is concealed from most everyone; this Wisdom can only be revealed to select kabbalists by Divine revelation through a teacher, an angel, or Elijah the Prophet. See also: Concealed Torah, Revealed Torah, *Ta'amei Torah*

Something Out of Nothing – In the 99% Realm of the Creator, where there is no physicality, it is the norm to create Something Out of Nothing because there is nothing there to begin with. This is how the world was created.

Something Out of Something – In the 1% Realm—this physical world—where our five senses and the universal laws of physics limit us, it is impossible to create something out of nothing. We can only create something when we have something else to work from.

Soul – See: *Neshama*

Speaking Kingdom – There are four Kingdoms (Inanimate, Vegetative, Animal, and Speaking) that describe an individual's level of consciousness as well as the intensity of their Desire to Receive. Humans have the greatest Desire to Receive of any creation, and they are referred to in this Kingdom as those who can speak. Humans are unique in that they can use the power of the spoken world both to create and destroy. This is the highest level of Desire out of the four Kingdoms. See also: Animal Kingdom, Inanimate Kingdom, Vegetative Kingdom

Ta'amei Torah – The revealed wisdom of Kabbalah and the Torah. All secrets and teachings of Kabbalah and the Torah can be divided into two categories: *Sitrei Torah* and *Ta'amei Torah*. *Ta'amei Torah* (lit. Taste or Meaning of the Torah) refers to the teachings of the Torah where there is a clear and understandable explanation for each connection we make in our daily life through studying and performing the Precepts. These teachings are usually not concealed and are made known to everyone. See also: Concealed Torah, Revealed Torah, *Sitrei Torah*

Tana'im – The term for the kabbalists of the first and second centuries CE (singular, *Tana*). The spiritual teachings of the *Tana'im* were compiled into the many volumes of the *Mishnah*.

Ten Luminous Emanations (TLE) – The study of the emanations of the *Sefirot* from the Endless down to our physical world, compiled into seven volumes. This study, written by Rav Yehuda Ashlag, founder of The Kabbalah Centre, is vital for any deep understanding of the *Zohar* and of the way our universe functions. See also: *Sefirot*

Teshuvah – See: Repentance

Tetragrammaton – The four-letter combination of the Name of God, spelled out with the letters *Yud, Hei, Vav,* and *Hei*. This is the Name of God that denotes absolute mercy and sharing.

This World – The physical world that we live in, where we are subject to the laws of cause and effect and are bound by the limitations of time, space, and motion. Also called the 1% Realm, the 1% Reality, and the illusionary world. See also: World to Come, World of Action

Thought of Creation – The exact point in time when the Vessel, which the Creator had imbued with the Desire to Receive, resisted the Light and said, "Let me earn it." This was the thought that created the physical realm we live in. See also: Bestow Goodness

Tiferet (Beauty) –

1. The sixth of the ten *Sefirot* (levels). *Tiferet* emphasizes the ultimate representation of the Central Column, since this *Sefira* is found between *Chesed* and *Gevurah*, the representatives of the ultimate Right (Mercy) and ultimate Left (Judgment) Columns, respectively. The Chariot for the *Sefira* of *Tiferet* is Jacob the Patriarch. See also: *Chesed, Gevurah, Sefirot*

2. ***Tiferet*** is also used to describe something else: *Zeir Anpin* (Small Face), a code for the bundle of the lower six (out of ten) *Sefirot*: *Chesed* (Mercy), *Gevurah* (Judgment/ Might), *Tiferet* (Beauty), *Netzach* (Eternity/Victory), *Hod* (Glory), *Yesod* (Foundation). These six *Sefirot* are tightly enfolded within each other, compacted in a dimension that corresponds to the World of Creation. See also: Chest, World of Creation

Tikkun (Correction) – The process by which we correct, cleanse, and elevate our souls. We came to this world to "correct" the selfish aspects of our nature and to transform ourselves into "beings of sharing." Thus, everything we experience in life—good or bad— is a *Tikkun*, or correction, process. The purpose of this process is to bring every human being, along with the entire universe, to perfection. The process is also known as "karma" and "the purpose of reincarnation." See also: 6000 Years of *Tikkun*

Tikkunei HaZohar (*Corrections to the Zohar*) – This book addresses the same general subject matter as the *Zohar*, but it is written as 72 commentaries on *"Beresheet,"* the first word of the *Book of Genesis*. *Tikkunei HaZohar* discourses upon teachings specifically directed to the Age of Aquarius. This is the first learning that Rav Shimon bar Yochai received in the cave. See also: Rav Shimon bar Yochai, *Zohar*

Torah – The *Five Books of Moses*. Sometimes the entire body of biblical study—including the *Five Books of Moses*, the 24 other books of the Bible, the *Mishnah*, the *Talmud*, and Kabbalah—is referred to as the Torah.

Tip of the Letter Yud – Hebrew letters, when written in the *Ashurit* font, can have little "crowns" on top—lines and dots that extend above the top of the letter. In the letter *Yud* of the Tetragrammaton, there is a singular crown, and it represents the *Sefira* of *Keter*, the highest of the Ten *Sefirot*. See also: Tetragrammaton

Tractate – The *Talmud* and *Mishnah* are each split into six sections, with each of their six sections further divided into subsections called *masechet* or tractates. Each subsection is given a name that describes its topic of discussion.

Tractate *Avot* (Fathers) – Also known as *Pirkei Avot* (*Lessons of Our Fathers*), this is one of the very few tractates in the *Mishnah* that does not have a *Gemara* commentary on it. This tractate consists of ethical and moral principles and wise sayings to live by.

Tractate *Bava Kama* (First Gate) – This tractate discusses damages and compensation relating to property or personal belongings. The laws that are covered in Tractate *Bava Kama* are found in Exodus 21:18-19 and 21:24-22:5.

Tractate *Berachot* (Blessings) – This tractate discusses the prayers we say every day as well as the blessings we say throughout the day over food and drink.

Tractate *Kidushin* (Betrothal) – This tractate discusses the laws pertaining to the betrothal of a woman.

Tractate *Pesachim* (Passover) – This tractate discusses the sacrificial offering of *Pesach* (Passover) as well as all the laws regarding this holiday.

Tractate *Sanhedrin* (Assembly) – This tractate discusses criminal law, its proceedings, and its punishments. Tractate *Sanhedrin* is noteworthy as being a precursor to the development of modern-day common law principles.

Tractate *Shabbat* (Sabbath) – This tractate discusses the laws of *Shabbat*.

Tractate *Ta'anit* (Fasting) – This tractate discusses the laws of fast days and the proceedings and prayers involved.

Tractate *Ukatzim* (Stems) – This tractate in the *Mishnah* discusses the laws pertaining to the impurity that is found in the stems or peels of fruits and vegetables. There is no *Gemara* commentary on this tractate.

Tractate Yevamot (Weddings) – This tractate in the *Mishnah* and *Gemara* discusses the laws of *Yevamot*. *Yevamot* is a Precept that states that when a married man passes away without children, his brother shall marry the widow and have children so that the family name may be continued; this concept is also known as "levirate marriage."

Tree of Knowledge – The Tree of Knowledge of Good and Evil that is mentioned in the Torah is actually a metaphor for connecting to the physical reality and our ego, where we rely in our five physical senses instead of going beyond them and connecting to the 99% Realm of the Light. It enables us to have the free choice between Good and Evil, between the Light and our selfish behaviors. See also: Free Will, *Ruach*, World of Action

Tree of Life – The Tree of Life mentioned in the Torah is a metaphor for the Flawless Universe beyond the 1% Realm of our physical reality. This world is the 99% Realm that connects us to the Light and to becoming like God.

Tree of Life, The – The book that reveals the process of Creation and the secrets of the universe. *The Tree of Life* was written by Rav Isaac Luria (the Ari) in the 16th century. See also: Ari

Understanding – See: *Binah*

Vegetative Kingdom – One of the four Kingdoms (Inanimate, Vegetative, Animal, and Speaking), the Vegetative Kingdom is the second level, with a more intense Desire to Receive than the Inanimate, but less than the Animal and Speaking Kingdoms.

Vessel – The Desire to Receive in those whom the Creator created.

Way of Suffering – When we refuse to acknowledge our negative behaviors and proactively change our nature, we go through a cleansing process that is filled with chaos, pain, and suffering. In effect, if we do not change our nature on our own, the change will happen by force and will come about through physical suffering and pain.

Way of Torah – When we proactively change our nature and work on ourselves and our negative traits, we will cleanse our negativity away without any real pain and suffering. It is the easy way to accomplish change, one where only our ego will get hurt, not our soul.

Wisdom – See: *Chochmah*

Wisdom of Truth – Another term for the Wisdom of Kabbalah, so called because truth is something that is neither subjective nor inconsistent. Truth is a constant and does not change because of human influences.

World (*Olam*) – A World is a spiritual structure of five *Partzufim*. There are five *Sefirot* or channels that bring the Light down to this mundane reality. When these channels are filled with Light, we call them Worlds. Every World represents a different level of consciousness that is related to a level of the veil that covers the Light. The word *olam* in English means "disappearance," referring to the fact that only when the Light is clothed can a reality be revealed. The worlds are: Primordial Man (*Adam Kadmon*), Emanation (*Atzilut*), Creation (*Beriah*), Formation (*Yetzirah*), and Action (*Asiyah*). See also: Clothing, *Partzuf*, World of Action, World of Creation, World of Emanation, World of Formation

World of Action (*Asiyah*) – The lowest of the Five Spiritual Worlds that emerged after the *Tzimtzum* (Contraction) of the Vessel in the Endless. The World of Action is the dimension where the least amount of Light is revealed. This enables human beings to exercise their free will in discerning between good and evil. This World is also related to the *Sefira* of *Malchut* (Kingdom) and is referred to as the Tree of Knowledge of Good and Evil. Our physical world is at the bottom of this world. See also: Free Will, *Malchut*, Tree of Knowledge, World

World of Creation (*Beriah*) – The World above the World of Formation (*Yetzirah*) of the Five Supernal Worlds that appeared after the *Tzimtzum* (Contraction). *Beriah* is related to the *Sefira* of

Binah (Understanding) and is a universal energy store. It is related to the Supernal Mother or spiritual "mother figure" and is almost completely protected from the *Klipot* (Shells). See also: *Binah, Klipot, Shechinah*, World

World of Emanation (*Atzilut*) – The World above the World of Creation (*Beriah*) of the Five Supernal Worlds that appeared after the *Tzimtzum* (Contraction). In this high and most exalted World, the Vessel is passive in relation to the Light, allowing the Light to flow without any agenda. *Atzilut* is related to the *Sefira* of *Chochmah* (Wisdom). It is completely protected from the *Klipot* (Shells). See also: *Chochmah, Klipot*, World

World of Formation (*Yetzirah*) – The World about the World of Action (*Asiyah*) of the Five Spiritual Worlds that appeared after the *Tzimtzum* (Contraction). Whereas in the lowest World (Action), evil is the predominant force, in the World of Formation, goodness is the predominant force. *Yetzirah* is related to the *Sefira* of *Zeir Anpin* (Small Face) and to the energy of the Shield of David. See also: World, *Zeir Anpin*

Worlds of Holiness - The worlds governed by the endless Light: *Adam Kadmon* (Primordial Man), *Atzilut* (Emanation), *Beriah* (Creation), *Yetzirah* (Formation), and *Asiyah* (Action).

Worlds of Impurity – The negative reality of the Other Side and the mirror image of the Worlds of Holiness. The Worlds of Impurity are governed by the Satan.

World to Come – A realm where only happiness, fulfillment, love, and joy exist—the 99% Realm of the Light of the Creator. The kabbalists explain that the World to Come exists in each and every moment of our lives. Every action of ours creates an effect that comes back to us either for good and for bad, and through the way we live our lives, we can create worlds according to our design. The World to Come is commonly referred to as "the reality of life-after-life." See also: This World

Work with the Creator – Fulfilling the Precepts of the Bible and following the path of the Creator.

Yechida (**Oneness**) – The fifth and final part of a person's soul, when the individual unites completely with the Light of the Creator. See also: *Chaya, Nefesh, Neshama, Ruach*

Yesod (**Foundation**) – The ninth of the Ten *Sefirot* (levels). *Yesod* is like a great reservoir or funnel feeding *Malchut* with Light manageable for us to handle. *Yesod* is the ultimate representation of sustenance and abundance. The Chariot for the *Sefira* of *Yesod* is Joseph the Righteous, who provided sustenance and abundance from Egypt to the whole world during a famine, as described in the Book of Genesis. *Yesod* or Joseph is the link between the physical world and spiritual reality. See also: *Malchut, Sefirot*

Yetzirah – See: World of Formation

Zohar – The major work of Kabbalah. Written by the great sage Rav Shimon bar Yochai in the second century BCE, this 23-volume work is the basis and source of all the teachings of Kabbalah we have today. See also: Concealed Torah, Rav Shimon bar Yochai, Wisdom of Truth

More Ways to Bring the Wisdom of Kabbalah into your Life

The Wisdom of Truth: 12 Essays by the Holy Kabbalist Rav Yehuda Ashlag
Edited by Michael Berg

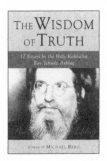

All of the essential truths of Kabbalah are encapsulated in these thought-provoking essays by arguably the most profound mystic of the 20th century. Originally published in 1984 as Kabbalah: A Gift of the Bible, and long out of print, this is a new translation from the Hebrew, edited and with an introduction by noted Kabbalah scholar Michael Berg.

And You Shall Choose Life: An Essay on Kabbalah, The Purpose of Life, and Our True Spiritual Work
By Rav Ashlag, Edited by Michael Berg

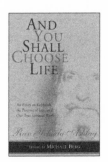

Preceding the time this essay was written in 1933-34, Kabbalah was considered taboo. But Rav Ashlag, the founder of The Kabbalah Centre, was a visionary pioneer. This book gives insight into one of the greatest kabbalistic thought leaders of all time. One of the most challenging aspects is the tone of urgency. As people were swept up in pain and suffering, Rav Ashlag tried to explain that despite outer events, the Creator is good. "Choosing life" means forming a connection to God, removing ego and pursuing the spiritual path of Kabbalah. Although written many decades ago, the essays are timeless.

On World Peace
By Rav Ashlag
Edited by Michael Berg

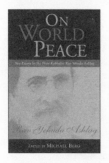

Everything that exists in reality, whether good or bad—including even the most evil and damage-causing thing in the world—has the right to exist, to the degree that destroying it and removing it completely from the world is forbidden. Rather, our duty is to only repair or fix it and to guide it towards goodness, for even a casual observation of any sort at the work of Creation that lies before us is enough [for us] to infer the high degree of perfection of Him Who has created it.

In these short but powerful treatises, Rav Ashlag explains that evil (or that which is not good), is nothing more than a work in progress and that seeing something as evil is no more relevant than judging an unripe fruit before it's time. He awakens us to the knowledge that upon arrival at our final destination *all things*, even the most damaged will be good.

This remarkable perspective helps us to view with awe the system the Creator has given us to develop and grow, and to gain certainty in the end of the journey. How will the process work? For this information, you'll want read the second essay, *One Precept* and experience for yourself the route to consciousness that Rav Ashlag so aptly charts out for us.

As the handwriting of a righteous person contains spiritual energy, *On World Peace* includes copies of Rav Ashlag's original writings. The book is nothing less than a gift to humanity.

Beloved of My Soul: Letters from Rav Brandwein to Rav Berg
Edited by Michael Berg

It is said the greatest love exists between a student and his spiritual teacher. In a bond of study, their hearts and consciousness are united. As these two souls on a path converge, they carry the lineage of previous masters, and ignite the way for future generations of students. This book is a rare glimpse into such a relationshipThrough the 37 letters presented here, written from Rav Brandwein to Rav Berg between 1965 and 1969, we gain deep insights into loving spiritual lessons from teacher to student. The letters are presented without a filter of interpretation, allowing readers to leave with answers—and more questions—and a yearning for greater wisdom. Rav Brandwein always instructed Rav Berg to review each letter at least three times and see what he could derive to help with his own service of God.

Secrets of the Zohar: Stories and Meditations to Awaken the Heart
By Michael Berg

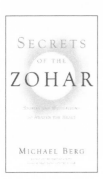

The Zohar's secrets are the secrets of the Bible, passed on as oral tradition and then recorded as a sacred text that remained hidden for thousands of years. They have never been revealed quite as they are here in these pages, which decipher the codes behind the best stories of the ancient sages and offer a special meditation for each one. Entire portions of the Zohar are presented, with the Aramaic and its English translation in side-by-side columns. This allows you to scan and to read aloud so that you can draw on the Zohar's full energy and achieve spiritual transformation. Open this book and open your heart to the Light of the Zohar!

The *Zohar*

Composed more than 2,000 years ago, the 23-volume *Zohar* is a commentary on biblical and spiritual matters written in the form of conversations among teachers. It was given to all humankind by the Creator to bring us protection, to connect us with the Creator's Light, and ultimately to fulfill our birthright of transformation. The *Zohar* is an effective tool for achieving our purpose in life.

More than eighty years ago, when The Kabbalah Centre was founded, the *Zohar* had virtually disappeared from the world. Today, all this has changed. Through the editorial efforts of Michael Berg, the *Zohar* is available in the original Aramaic language and for the first time in English with commentary.

We teach Kabbalah, not as a scholarly study but as a way of creating a better life and a better world.

WHO WE ARE

The Kabbalah Centre is a non-profit organization that makes the principles of Kabbalah understandable and relevant to everyday life. The Kabbalah Centre teachers provide students with spiritual tools based on kabbalistic principles that students can then apply as they see fit to improve their own lives and by doing so, make the world better. The Centre was founded by Rav Yehuda Ashlag in 1922 and now spans the globe with brick-and-mortar locations in more than 40 cities as well as an extensive online presence. To learn more, visit www.kabbalah.com.

WHAT WE TEACH

There are five core principles:

- **Sharing:** Sharing is the purpose of life and the only way to truly receive fulfillment. When individuals share, they connect to the force of energy that Kabbalah calls the Light—the Infinite Source of Goodness, the Divine Force, the Creator. By sharing, one can overcome ego—the force of negativity.

- **Awareness and Balance of the Ego:** The ego is a voice inside that directs people to be selfish, narrow-minded, limited, addicted, hurtful, irresponsible, negative, angry, and hateful. The ego is a main source of problems because it allows us to believe that others are separate from us. It is the opposite of sharing and humility. The ego also has a positive side, as it motivates one to take action. It is up to each individual to choose whether they act for themselves or whether to also act in the well-being of others. It is important to be aware of one's ego and to balance the positives and negatives.

- **Existence of Spiritual Laws:** There are spiritual laws in the universe that affect people's lives. One of these is the Law of Cause and Effect: What one puts out is what one get back, or what we sow is what we reap.

- **We Are All One:** Every human being has within him- or herself a spark of the Creator that binds each and every person into one totality. This understanding informs us of the spiritual precept that every human being must be treated with dignity at all times, under any circumstances. Individually, everyone is responsible for war and poverty in all parts of the world and individuals can't enjoy true and lasting fulfillment as long as others are suffering.

- **Leaving Our Comfort Zone Can Create Miracles:** Becoming uncomfortable for the sake of helping others taps us into a spiritual dimension that ultimately brings Light and positivity to our lives.

HOW WE TEACH

Courses and Classes. On a daily basis, The Kabbalah Centre focuses on a variety of ways to help students learn the core kabbalistic principles. For example, The Centre develops courses, classes, online lectures, books, and audio products. Online courses and lectures are critical for students located around the world who want to study Kabbalah but don't have access to a Kabbalah Centre in their community. To learn more, visit www.ukabbalah.com.

Spiritual Services and Events. The Centre organizes and hosts a variety of weekly and monthly events and spiritual services where students can participate in lectures, meditation and share meals together. Some events are held through live streaming online. The Centre organizes spiritual retreats and tours to energy sites, which are places that have been closely touched by great kabbalists. For example, tours take place at locations where kabbalists may have studied or been buried, or where ancient texts like the *Zohar* were authored. International events provide students from all over the world with an opportunity to make connections to unique energy available at certain times of the year. At these events, students meet with other students, share experiences and build friendships.

Volunteering. In the spirit of Kabbalah's principles that emphasize sharing, The Centre provides a volunteer program so that students can participate in charitable initiatives, which includes sharing the wisdom of Kabbalah itself through a mentoring program. Every year, hundreds of student volunteers organize projects that benefit their communities such as feeding the homeless, cleaning beaches and visiting hospital patients.

One-on-One. The Kabbalah Centre seeks to ensure that each student is supported in his or her study. Teachers and mentors are part of the educational infrastructure that is available to students 24 hours a day, seven days a week.

Hundreds of teachers are available worldwide for students as well as a study program for their continued development. Study takes place in person, by phone, in study groups, through webinars, and even self-directed study in audio format or online.

Kabbalah University (ukabbalah.com). Kabbalah University (ukabbalah.com) is an online university providing lectures, courses, and events in English and Spanish. This is an important link for students in the United States and around the globe, who want to study Kabbalah but don't have access to a Kabbalah Centre in their community. Kabbalah University offers a library of wisdom spanning 30 years. This virtual Kabbalah Centre presents the same courses and spiritual connections as the physical centers with an added benefit of streaming videos from worldwide events.

Kabbalah.com. Kabbalah.com is the leading online source for learning the teachings of Kabbalah. Serving as an extension of The Kabbalah Centre's mission, Kabbalah.com provides students with spiritual tools based on kabbalistic principals that people of all races, religions and backgrounds can apply as they see fit to not only benefit themselves, but to help make the world a better place.

To support the learning needs of The Kabbalah Centre's global community, Kabbalah.com includes access to online video and audio courses, live streaming events, articles, as well as online access to the 23 volume Zohar, the primary book of kabbalistic wisdom.

Visitors to Kabbalah.com can also connect with students around the world through a number of interactive features.

Whether you are new to the teachings of The Kabbalah Centre or have been a student for any period of time, we welcome you to discover all that Kabbalah.com has to offer.

Publishing. Each year, The Centre translates and publishes some of the most challenging kabbalistic texts for advanced scholars including the *Zohar*, *Writings of the Ari*, and the *Ten Luminous Emanations with Commentary*. Drawing from these sources The Kabbalah Centre publishes books yearly in more than 30 languages that are tailored for both beginner- and intermediate-level students and distributed around the world.

Zohar Project. The *Zohar*, the primary text of kabbalistic wisdom, is a commentary on biblical and spiritual matters composed and compiled over 2000 years ago and is believed to be a source of Light. Kabbalists believe that when it is brought into areas of darkness and turmoil, the *Zohar* can create change and bring about improvement. The Kabbalah Centre's *Zohar* Project shares the *Zohar* in 95 countries by distributing free copies to organizations and individuals in recognition of their service to the community and to areas where there is danger. In the past year, over 50,000 copies of the *Zohar* were donated to hospitals, embassies, places of worship, universities, not-for-profit organizations, emergency services, war zones, natural disaster locations, soldiers, pilots, government officials, medical professionals, humanitarian aid workers, and more.

To my grandmother

Sara bat Ishileib Valdman

Like Rachel, she only cared about the well being of others.

She was always sharing, giving and loving.

Her family and friends always came first.